BLOODSHOT
— AND —
BROKEN

TRISHA TILLMAN

Fulton Books
Meadville, PA

Published by Fulton Books 2022

ISBN 979-8-88505-668-7 (paperback)
ISBN 979-8-88505-669-4 (digital)

Printed in the United States of America

To anyone who has suffered the effects of addiction, physical and emotional abuse, or the loss of a loved one. I also want to dedicate it in memory of my mother (especially the very last sentence).

PROLOGUE

Just like clockwork, every single night, I was waking up crying hysterically. It would start out as a dream that I could never quite remember once I was sat up in bed, screaming as tears streamed down my face, crying for something, for someone. For who or what, I wasn't sure whether it was someone who hurt me or someone I missed, someone I loved or someone I hated, someone I was longing for, or someone I was desperately trying to get away from. But one thing I was sure of was that my heart was remembering things that my mind could not. And it was slowly tearing me apart.

This was the only life I knew. I had one before. Whether it was good or bad, I don't know. But I do know I had one. But since I had no memory of it, this life of terror and never-ending questions was the only normal I knew. Who was I? Where did I come from? Did I have family? I didn't even know if I was good or bad. So many secrets buried in my past. Maybe I was a spy, maybe an FBI agent, maybe I volunteered at an animal shelter, or maybe I was just the most boring person on the planet and lived with my fifty cats in a nine-hundred-square-foot apartment. Or maybe I was a criminal on the run from the law, always taking refuge in random locations, sure to never be discovered. All of them were possible. But to be honest, none of them felt right. None of them felt like me. But even if I didn't like who I was, I just needed to know the truth. But the chances of that happening seemed to slip farther and farther away as each day passed. And the fear of the unknown and the possibility of never knowing was completely swallowing me whole as I sank deeper and deeper into this whirlpool of desperation, anxiety, and insomnia.

CHAPTER 1

October 1, 2014

Julia

What is that beeping noise? Why do I feel like my eyelids are so heavy that I physically can't open them? Why are my feet numb? I'm freezing. Why is it so cold? Where am I? Wait. Who am I? What is my name? Why can't I remember my name? Am I dead? Is that why? When you die, do you just automatically forget your name? That's it. I'm dead. I can hear voices, but I don't know what they are saying. They must be taking me to Jesus. Wait. Is that good? Am I even going to heaven? I don't know who I am! Am I even a good person? I have to open my eyes. I have to see what's around me. Wait. I think I did it. I see light. Yes, blinding light. This is it. This is the end. Whoever I am, I'm leaving this earth right now.

"Julia, can you hear me?"

Wait, who was that? Are they talking to me? Is that the head angel or the grim reaper? No, her voice is too soft to be the grim reaper. She must be an angel. Is she asking if I can hear her? Am I Julia?

"Julia, I'm right here. Can you look at me?"

Okay, someone just grabbed my hand. And I felt it. So maybe I'm not dead. Wait. I can see the lights better now. Am I in a hospital? Yes. That must be it. I'm hurt, not dead. So if this is not an angel, who is it? I have to see her face. If I can just slightly turn my head. Oh, there she is. She looks nice. She's smiling. She seems happy to see me. I don't know who she is, though. Hell, I don't even know who I am, much less anybody else. Why does my head hurt so bad? What happened? I need to speak these words instead of just think them. Can I talk?

"Wha... Wh..."

"It's okay, Julia. I'm here. You were in an accident—a car wreck. It banged you up pretty badly. You were in a medically induced coma for three days. There was so much swelling on your brain. We weren't sure. Well, we weren't sure what to expect when you woke up. Do you remember anything?"

This is too much. I want answers, but damn, that's a lot to take in all at once. I think I'll look back up at the light before she feels the need to say anything else.

Oh no, I hear more people coming. She must have alerted the media that I'm awake. I just want them to go away. I want all this to go away. I just want to wake up knowing who I am and in my own bed, wherever that is.

"Julia, it's nice to see you awake. I'm Dr. Roberts. You gave us quite the scare there, young lady. How are you feeling?"

I'm sure to give the meanest look I can manage in hopes that he will just go away and take the rest of them with him. I think I'll just go back to my coma now if you all don't mind.

The doctor then proceeds to shine a tiny bright light straight into my eyes and then moves his finger back and forth in front of my face, asking me to follow it with my eyes. I do so lazily, then blink hard to get rid of the blindness that the light has left behind. "Do you feel like answering a few questions for me, Julia?" he asks, smiling brightly. I slowly close my eyes and turn my head, dismissing his request.

"Ah, I see. Not in the mood to talk, huh. That's okay. Take your time. But as soon as you're feeling up to it, I'll need to evaluate you to see just how much damage has been done. Go ahead and get some rest for now, okay? See you soon."

Good riddance. If I find a way out of here before then, you won't see me at all. I'm not sure why I'm so angry at everyone. I know they are all just trying to help. But I can't help it. Anger is all I know to feel right now other than fear. And I'm not sure I can handle fear at the moment, so I'm going to stick with anger for now. I just want to close my eyes and make all this go away.

October 2, 2014

I must have fallen asleep. For how long, I'm not sure. But I feel a little stronger. My eyes are opening easier now. It's early in the morning. The lights are off in the room, and the sun is barely creeping through the darkness outside. This is much more pleasant than the bright-white light I woke up to before. There's that woman, the one that was here when I woke up the first time. She's sleeping on the small couch next to my bed. The small blanket pulled over her has fallen and is mostly hanging to the floor instead of covering her up. I wonder how long she has been in my room. I wonder if I can lift my hands. I'll start slow. I'll try moving my fingers first.

I did it. Okay, now I'll try squeezing my hand. Did that too. Okay, now I'm going to lift it, even if just a couple of inches. I did it! I knew I felt stronger. Now if I could just get out of this bed. Everything feels so stiff, but I've managed to slightly wiggle around and spark life into my body. Uh-oh, the woman is waking up. Busted.

"Julia? Wha… What are you doing?" she says, yawning.

She's standing over me now, gently grabbing my arm with one hand and stroking my hair with the other.

I think I can talk today. I'm sure of it. Maybe this nice woman will help me get out of here.

"I wa… I want to leave," I manage to stammer.

"Oh, Julia, you have a long recovery ahead of you. You'll be here for a while until you're strong enough to care for yourself," she says, smiling with sympathy.

She speaks to me as if I am a child or like I'm a complete idiot. I feel like I should be able to get up and walk out of here as I please. But deep down inside, I know she's right. I barely just figured out how to move, how to speak. How am I going to leave? And where would I go? I don't even know where I live.

"Julia, do you remember anything about the night of your accident?"

She's really digging at me, trying to find out what's going on in this damaged brain of mine. It's like I'm a science project, another medical mystery. They can't wait to poke and pry at me and study me and examine me. But maybe they should remember I am a person, not just another medical case for them to solve.

"I don't remember anything about that or anything else. I don't know who I am. I don't know where I came from. Do you know who I am other than my name?" I ask this hopefully, knowing she probably doesn't know. I probably had some type of identification on me that told them what my name was. Other than that, this woman doesn't know anything about me. I'm just another patient to her. I look at the despair that comes over her face. Tears are forming in her eyes. She wipes casually at them as she starts to speak.

"Um, no. No, I'm sorry. I just, um, I was really hoping that this wouldn't be the outcome for you, even though the doctor said it was possible. So you don't remember anything or anybody?"

"No. Nothing. The only reason I know my name is because you keep saying it to me."

"I am so sorry, Julia. Don't worry. We are going to take good care of you. Everything will be okay," she says while trying to convince herself as well.

"Why are you always in my room? Who are you?" I ask in the nicest way I can manage.

"My name is Anna. I was assigned to be your nurse to sit with you and take care of you. Someone with the amount of head trauma that you have suffered has to be watched constantly."

"Oh, well, thank you for watching me. I guess I can speak with the doctor now."

CHAPTER 2

October 6, 2014

The past few days have been a whirlwind of tests, questions, crying, and vomiting. I don't know what my life was like before this, but I feel pretty certain that this is the worst thing I have ever gone through.

Anna has been great. I have really come to like her. She has been by my side the whole time, except for the few hours she leaves in the evenings. I have made enough progress to be left alone in my room for short periods. Anna says she has taken on extra shifts just to stay and care for me. We have bonded, almost as if we have become friends. She seems to really care about me. I wonder if she cares for all her patients this much. It may sound stupid, but I feel like she's all I have. She's the closest thing to a friend that I have right now, and honestly, I dread the day they release me from this hospital and I'm forced to leave her. I don't have anybody else. I'm sure she will just move on to the next patient and forget that I ever existed, but I will truly miss her. I will be all alone. Just poor, pathetic Julia who doesn't know who she is—who has no life, no friends, no family. The girl who had a wreck and lived physically but died mentally. And my past died too. I've asked Anna to try to find out who I am and where I came from based on the belongings that were with me. But there wasn't much to work with. The car I wrecked was found engulfed in flames, and I was found walking aimlessly down the road with my eyes closed, blood gushing from my head.

I don't know much about myself, but one thing I do know is that I seem to like to try to get up and walk away when I'm not physically in the state of doing so.

October 9, 2014

I have been awake for a little over a week now. Dr. Roberts plans to release me tomorrow as long as I continue to show improvement today. Or at least that's what they call it, releasing me. But it feels more like I'm being kicked out, thrown out into the wild to fend for myself—lost and broken and alone out in the big, scary world. No home to go to, or not one that I remember anyway. No one waiting to hug me when I return. No money. No friends. Nothing. Just me. I'm not sure what is more terrifying: first waking up to all this or the thought of being all by myself with nowhere to go. I sit silently as the thoughts circle my mind over and over again. A single tear slides down my cheek and I quickly wipe it away when I see Anna walking in my room.

"Knock, knock!" she says cheerfully, tapping her knuckle on the door. I have failed to hide my worry. I know because I immediately see her expression change. "Oh, Julia, what's wrong, sweetie?" she says sympathetically as she rushes to my side. I put both hands to my face, trying to hold it all in. But instead, it comes gushing out of me, like water bursting through a broken levee.

"I'm being released tomorrow. I have nowhere to go! I don't know who I am! I'm going to be homeless! I'm so scared." My sobbing continues uncontrollably and builds higher and higher until Anna reaches and grabs my hand.

"Julia, stop. Look at me. Just listen, please. Try to calm down. That's what I came to talk to you about."

That last part really catches my attention. She's found something. She knows who I am. Anna has solved the mystery and she is going to send me home to my family. I slow my sobs and wipe my face, looking at her desperately, willing her to say the words. But what she says is not quite what I expect.

"Julia, I've grown quite attached to you over this past week. I would even say that we have become friends. I know you don't have anyone, and the truth is I really don't either. It's just me and my daughter at home. I would like to take you home with me, help you get better. You could stay as long as you want or need. Living alone with a baby can get kind of lonely sometimes. I would love the company. I have asked to take some time off so that I can stay home with you for a while. I want to help you through this, if you will let me."

I gasp in shock. I can't believe what she is saying. How could she be willing to do this for a complete stranger? I want so badly to jump up and scream *yes* to the top of my lungs. But I feel so pathetic having someone I barely know take off work, bring me into her home, and care for me. How disgusted my past self would have been having to be cared for like this, having to be so dependent. But this offer is too good to pass up. It's my only choice, really. This or be homeless.

"Anna, are you sure? That's a lot to ask of someone I've only known for a few days. I would completely disrupt your whole life."

She shakes her head assuringly and says, "You will not be disrupting anything, I promise. I want to help you. And besides, you're not asking. I'm offering, insisting really. In fact, I will absolutely not take no for an answer," she says, smiling.

"Anna, thank you. Thank you so much. I don't know what to say. I am forever grateful. I promise I will do my best to not be any trouble. And as soon as I'm well enough, I will get out on my own. Get a job. Do whatever it is that normal adults do. I promise."

She smiles assuringly and hugs me tightly. "Let's just get you well for now. Everything else will come with time."

CHAPTER 3

October 10, 2014

Anna is telling her coworkers goodbye as she pushes me down the long hospital hallway. They also tell me goodbye and wish me well. I'm not sure what to expect when I am outside these cold, white walls that have held me captive, all while keeping me safe. I don't remember what the world is like. I don't remember what normal life is like. And I don't remember what home feels like, but I hope that Anna's home will soon feel like mine as well and not like I am a stranger intruding in her well-established life. We finally make it outside and head toward her silver Honda. The air is fresh and crisp around me as I breathe it in. She asks if I need help getting into the car, but I tell her I can manage. I am feeling good physically at this point. I don't have any trouble standing or walking, and even my head has stopped throbbing. The only thing that is left broken is my mind.

Going down the road, I stare out the window as I take in every single detail that passes us by. Nothing seems familiar.

Anna breaks the silence suddenly as I slightly jump and turn to face her.

"I can't wait for you to meet my little girl. She is ten months old. Her name is Audrey. She's a sweetheart. You will love her," Anna promises, smiling cheerfully.

"What happened to her father?" I ask meekly, hoping I haven't overstepped my boundaries.

"Oh," she says, caught off guard. "He, um, well, he wasn't a very good man. He was abusive. He is no longer in our lives," she says, clearing her throat and quickly changing the subject. I want to say that I'm sorry for being nosy—that I had no right to ask. But she has already directed the conversation elsewhere, so I don't dare go back. "What do you want for dinner? I don't really have many groceries to cook, but we can order takeout or pizza. Anything you want," she asks cheerfully, trying to kill the tension that was with us seconds before.

"Anything is fine with me, Anna. I'm just so thankful to even have food and not be living on the streets right now," I say, smiling gratefully at her.

A few minutes later, we pull into her driveway. It's a small, cottage-style home with lots of flowers surrounding the front. We pull around back and she hurries around to open my door and ask once again if I need help. We make our way to the back door and a woman somewhere close to mine and Anna's age greets us at the door.

"Hey, you must be Julia. It's so nice to finally meet you! How are you feeling? My name is Gracie," she says cheerfully, holding out her hand. I shake her hand and smile, not nearly as excited to meet her as she is me.

"I, um, I'm doing okay," I say as we make our way into Anna's home.

"Gracie is my best friend. We've been close ever since elementary school. She was watching Audrey for me until I got home," Anna says. "Speaking of whom, you need to meet right now!" She says excitedly.

"I will let myself out," Gracie says, smiling at Anna. "Call me later!" She says as she closes the door.

We make our way into the living room and Anna hurries over to pick the baby girl up from a pallet that is covered in toys, spilled snacks, and fruit-juice stains. She walks over to me and turns the baby toward me so I can get a good look. "Julia, this is Audrey," she says, beaming with joy. As I look at the baby, I wonder to myself if I would ever be well enough to have children of my own. Would I ever learn who I was or where I had been before now? Would I ever be able to take care of myself, much less a child? Or would I live the rest of my life wandering aimlessly, lost, broken, and confused—not much more capable than a child myself? I'm not sure if I even liked children. I had no memory of ever being around them—whether I thought they were cute or whether they unnerved me. But the way this baby looks at me and something about her soft, chubby skin and her toothless grin comfort me.

"Would you like to hold her?" Anna asks. Startled, I jump back, holding my hands up in defense.

"No. No, I don't think so," I say quickly to stop her from bringing her closer. But that doesn't seem to stop her at all.

She comes closer to me, holding the chubby baby out toward me and insists, "Come on. She won't bite. Holding a baby makes everyone feel a little better."

I am prepared to dart across the room to escape the pressure of holding this woman's child. But suddenly, the baby holds out her chubby hands to me and smiles, gurgling bubbles and giggling as if she thinks my reaction is somehow humorous. And suddenly, there is something about her that I can no longer resist. Without thinking it through, I reach my arms out to retrieve her, wondering if I even knew how to hold a baby, if I ever even had held a baby. But even if I don't know what I am doing, she seems to know exactly what to do. She immediately sinks into my arms and reaches for my face as if to examine everything to make sure it is all placed properly. She giggles as she sticks a finger to my eye and causes me to jerk my head sideways. As I look down into her face and watch her bat her big, blue eyes at me, I decide, even if I didn't like babies before, I like this one.

I end up spending the entire evening playing and laughing with Audrey. Maybe she is like this with everyone, but I can't help to believe that she really likes me. I feel so at ease with her, so comfortable. And I can't help but wonder, *Maybe I did have experience with children. Maybe I had a younger sibling growing up. Maybe I had a job babysitting in high school.* And then my next thought sends chills down my spine and causes me to shiver, *Was it possible that I could have had children of my own? What if they were left wondering why I never came home? Or worse, what if they were in the car with me the night I wrecked? The car that was engulfed in flames.* I try to shake the haunting thoughts from my mind, but still, they linger. Anna comes in the room, holding a cup with steam rising slowly.

"I made you some tea. It has chamomile and lavender. It should help you sleep much better than you have in that loud, cold hospital," she says, smiling and handing me the warm tea.

"Anna," I say blankly and pause for a moment. "I was alone that night, wasn't I? The night of the wreck. There wasn't anyone with me, right?" I ask slowly, fearing the answer she would give. A look of shock comes over her face for a split second and then it is gone.

"Oh no, honey, no one was with you. Try not to worry yourself. You're safe now. And I can see that you and Audrey are getting along great. We are so happy to have you here with us, Julia," she says, smiling.

And suddenly, I feel better. I feel like I really am safe. And in the short time I have known Anna and the even shorter time I have known Audrey, they feel like family. And this feels like home.

CHAPTER 4

July 3, 2017

Just like clockwork, every single night, I was waking up crying hysterically. It would start out as a dream that I could never quite remember once I was sat up in bed, screaming as tears streamed down my face, crying for something, for someone. For who or what, I wasn't sure whether it was someone who hurt me or someone I missed, someone I loved or someone I hated, someone I was longing for, or someone I was desperately trying to get away from. But one thing I was sure of was that my heart was remembering things that my mind could not. And it was slowly tearing me apart.

This was the only life I knew. I had one before. Whether it was good or bad, I don't know. But I do know I had one. But since I had no memory of it, this life of terror and never-ending questions was the only normal I knew. Who was I? Where did I come from? Did I have family? I didn't even know if I was good or bad. So many secrets buried in my past. Maybe I was a spy, maybe an FBI agent, maybe I volunteered at an animal shelter, or maybe I was just the most boring person on the planet and lived with my fifteen cats in a nine-hundred-square-foot apartment. Or maybe I was a criminal on the run from the law, always taking refuge in random locations, sure to never be discovered. All of them were possible. But to be honest, none of them felt right. None of them felt like me. But even if I didn't like who I was, I just needed to know the truth. But the chances of that happening seemed to slip farther and farther away as each day passed. And the fear of the unknown and the possibility of never knowing was completely swallowing me whole as I sank deeper and deeper into this whirlpool of desperation, anxiety, and insomnia.

I think back to my first night home with Anna and Audrey, how Anna had made me the tea and promised a good night's sleep, and how wrong she was. That was close to three years ago and I haven't had one peaceful night since. I love Anna and Audrey. They are my family now. But something inside me constantly aches uncontrollably and I know I have a past that remembers me, even if I can't remember it. It is tearing into my soul, begging me to uncover it, and I know it will never let me rest until I do just that.

A few months after going to live with Anna, I moved into the apartment above her garage. I enjoy the privacy, but part of me still longs to be in the house with her and Audrey. I still spend quite a good bit of time in the main house with them. We eat most of our meals together and spend lots of time together, but still, I miss fully living there with them. I am lonely without them. I had made the suggestion to clean out the apartment and move in after several nights of waking them both. My nightly hysterical screams had woken up Audrey, leaving Anna to deal with her crying for hours. This has happened more times than I like to think about. I felt horrible and I knew it couldn't continue. Anna assured me—with dark circles under her eyes from exhaustion—that it was fine and that I did not have to move to the apartment. But I wouldn't have it. She had already done so much for me. I couldn't keep her and her baby up every night.

July 4, 2017

We are having our yearly Fourth of July cookout. Our neighborhood is the best. Everyone on our street knows each other. Every year, we all get together and have one huge cookout. Kids are running and playing. The men are cooking on the grill. And me and Anna and our girlfriends are all sitting around, sipping cold drinks, talking, and laughing. It's moments like this that I almost forget I had a different life before. Moments like this just feel right. "Juwia! Juwia! It's time for the fireworks to start!" Audrey screams excitedly as she runs toward me and climbs into my lap. Me and Audrey are inseparable. I guess I'm kind of like her cool aunt in a sense. She absolutely adores me and the feeling is completely mutual. That little girl has my heart. I smile excitedly and throw my arms around her. "Well, we better hurry so we can get a good seat!" I say, tickling her and sending her into an uncontrollable, contagious laughter. She squeals and grabs my hand, jumping up and pulling me out of my chair. We all head to the row of seats that have been lined up in the backyard. There is a big firework show that a major company puts on every year and it just so happens that our backyard has the perfect view of the show. Someone has their truck pulled up with the radio turned on and the windows rolled down. A song comes on that sounds familiar to me, but I'm not sure where I've heard it. About that time, a small boy runs up behind us, setting off fireworks that shoot violently through the chairs and send several people running and screaming. Someone grabs my arm, and everything goes black. My eyes are open, but my surroundings have changed. I am not in the same place. I am not safe anymore. That song is playing even louder now, and the grip on my arm gets tighter. "You're hurting me," I try to say, but nothing comes out. "Dammit, Julia! Why do you always have to ruin everything? Just calm down and have fun for a change." I don't know who this is shouting at me. It's a man. He sounds angry and drunk. His speech is slurred, and I'm certain he's the one gripping my arm. "Let go. PLEASE," I mouth the words, but once again, no sound leaves my mouth. Fireworks are shooting all around me. I smell the smoke and feel as if I'm going to be sick. Suddenly, the hand releases my arm and is joined by another hand that shoves me hard with more force than I know how to fight. My reflexes go dormant as I struggle to catch myself. But just like my voice I have lost all control of my body. My arms are like Jell-O as I try desperately to grab something to break my fall. Suddenly, I feel the harsh force of the ground hit my entire body and then my head. The sounds and smells swirl around me as I try to find my way out of this nightmare.

"Julia? Julia! Wake up, Julia. Please, you're scaring me." I hear Anna's voice and slowly open my eyes as she shakes me gently. I see her face and it is clear that she is just as terrified as I am.

"Where did I just go? Who was I just with? Who was just grabbing my arm?" I ask her, looking around for the man that was just hurting me.

"Julia, sweetie. No one grabbed you. We were all just walking to our seats. Jeffrey accidentally let some fireworks get away from him, and suddenly, you were on the ground."

It's then that I hear sniffling and whimpering, and I recognize the sweet little voice behind it. I look around until I spot Audrey who has her hands to her face and is crying, terrified. "Audrey," I say, jumping up and running past the group of people standing around, staring. I grab her in my arms and hold her tightly. "I'm so sorry, Audrey. I'm so sorry. I didn't mean to scare you. I just… I just fell down. That's all. Everything is fine now." I turn to see Anna staring at me. There is a look in her eyes that I have never seen before. But just as I walk up to her to ask her what's wrong, she quickly changes her expression and smiles.

"Why don't I go get you some water? I'll be right back," she says, patting Audrey on the back and walking away quickly.

I decide to turn in early and skip the firework show. I go back to my apartment and sit quietly, trying to make sense of what happened. It was a memory. I'm sure of it. Something about that song playing along with the sound of the fireworks triggered me to remember something. My mind is racing with questions. Who was that man? Why was he so mad? Was he like that to me all the time? One thing I am sure of is that if he is all my past has to offer, maybe it is best I don't remember. Suddenly, I am thankful for the wreck. If it got me away from him and to Anna and Audrey, then it wasn't a bad thing at all. It was a blessing. And for a split second, I decide that I will leave my past behind me—that I will no longer wonder. Instead, I will be thankful. But then that overwhelming surge goes through my body once again, and I realize it is not him that my heart is missing. There is someone else. And now I want more than ever to find them. What if they are in danger? What if he is hurting them like he hurt me? A sense of desperation comes over me. And then that turns to motivation, which turns to determination. I *will* find him. And I will save whoever it is that I am missing from him. And I will not stop until I do.

CHAPTER 5

July 5, 2017

I wake up the next morning from my usual lack of sleep. As soon as my body starts relaxing, my mind immediately wakes it up, searching for those memories that were buried years ago. I walk into the bathroom and splash water on my face. Looking in the mirror, I see that my eyes are bloodshot, just as they are every morning. I see that in the last three years, I look as if I have aged ten. The thick, dirty-blond hair that filled my head before has dwindled down to pitiful thin strands that hang weakly over my shoulders. That brings my attention to how bony my shoulder is. I wasn't big before, but the stress and lack of sleep over these past three years has shrunk me down to skin and bones. I think maybe if your heart aches long enough, your body retaliates against you until you give it what it wants. I see what a mess I have become, this person staring back at me, bloodshot and broken and possibly unrepairable. But just as I decided last night, I will not stop until I find answers. Whatever secrets my past holds captive I will uncover and lay to rest, bringing whoever it is that I love and miss right along with me. That man may have scared me last night. But I was in a blackout. I couldn't defend myself. He doesn't scare me now. I have been through too much. I will not let him overpower me. He will never hurt me again.

I spend the next few hours searching frantically on the Internet, searching my name, searching news articles for the day of my wreck, searching missing people—all things that I have done countless times before. I find nothing. It just doesn't make sense. How could there be no reports of me vanishing? Even if this man from my past was a monster, wouldn't he have wondered where I was? I type my name in one last time and scan over the articles that I have already read countless times. But this time, I notice one that I hadn't before. It's a wedding announcement. I click on it. And there I am with a man. He doesn't look mean at all. In fact, we both look pretty happy. His arms are wrapped around my shoulders and his hands are connected right at my chest. My left hand is lifted and resting gently on his to reveal a stunning diamond ring on my finger that represents the upcoming commitment that we are posing in the picture for. We both have relaxed and natural smiles and seem to be simply young and in love. The article reads, "We are pleased to announce and celebrate the upcoming marriage of Mr. Benjamin Harris and Ms. Julia Owens. The ceremony will be held on July 17, 2012, at the Ridgemond Country Club with reception to follow immediately."

"Benjamin Harris," I whisper as I type violently and wait impatiently for the computer screen to give me more answers. A whole list of articles appears before me. But these don't seem to be such happy events.

January 1, 2013. A mug shot claiming Mr. Harris was arrested after police were notified of a domestic disturbance at a New Year's celebration. He was highly intoxicated and uncooperative as police arrived on the scene. He was released after making bond two days later.

March 5, 2013. It shows another domestic case, but this time, he tested positive for cocaine and became extremely violent with arresting officers.

April 17, 2013. DUI charges.

June 10, 2013. Possession of heroin.

And the list goes on and on, each mug shot looking less and less like the happy, smiling face from the engagement picture. It was like I was watching this man's life, my husband's life, spiral out of control right before my eyes. I continue to search through them until suddenly, they stop altogether around September 2014, which I realize is right around the time of my wreck. There is no trace of him whatsoever after that. And suddenly, I realize I am not the only one who vanished into thin air that night.

CHAPTER 6

November 30, 2017

My main focus these last few months has been Benjamin Harris—my husband, the man I don't remember, the criminal, the man that was mean to me, the man that hurt me.

But since the engagement photo and the ongoing list of mug shots, I haven't found anything else about him. It seems that he is just as untraceable as I am. My mind has circled around endless possibilities, but none of them bring me to any real answers. Today, I will try to push these thoughts aside. Today is for family. Today is for being thankful and stuffing myself full of food until I can't move. I don't remember any holiday traditions before the wreck, but since coming to live with Anna, it's always been the same every year. She makes the turkey. I attempt to make the dressing. And we each do our own surprise dessert to see who has the best one. We don't tell anyone attending dinner who made which dessert, and after everyone has tasted it, we take a vote to see who likes which one better. I took the trophy for the first time last year and I fully intend to keep it today. I will not let Benjamin Harris take my Thanksgiving happiness.

Anna walks into the kitchen and addresses me as if we are opponents in a battle.

"Julia," she sneers, playfully glaring at me.

"Anna," I return, turning my nose up and stirring viciously at my dessert mixture as I step to the side to be sure she doesn't sneak a peek at what I'm making.

We turn to each other and laugh as she points at me and says, "No way I'm letting you win two years in a row."

We laugh, talk, cook, and sip wine until our dinner party arrives promptly at six: Gracie comes with her husband; Anna's cousin David with his girlfriend; and our neighbor, Mrs. Atkins, who lives alone and has no family. We always try to include her in all family events so she doesn't feel lonely.

I look around the room and realize all these people, everyone gathered here to celebrate this holiday, are all Anna's people. I mean, sure, I have come to know and love them all over these past few years but only because I know Anna. There is not one single person in my life that I know for any reason other than them knowing Anna first. And then I look at sweet Audrey. I wonder how her father could just abandon her. How could he at least not call and tell her, "Happy Thanksgiving"? And then I realize that she, too, only knows everyone here because of Anna. And suddenly, I don't feel so bad. She catches me staring at her and smiles and runs toward me, reaching her arms up. I scoop her up and hug her tight.

"Happy Thanksgiving, little turkey," I joke, tickling her side. She giggles and hugs me back.

"I love you, Juwia."

My heart melts. If I never find anything about my past, this little girl's love makes my life worth living. I can't explain how much I care for her. Sometimes it doesn't make sense how someone else's child makes my heart beat faster, how I would literally die for her in a split second, and how I feel like I can't breathe when I'm not around her. I look around the room again, and suddenly, I really am thankful, thankful that my past sent me spiraling into this life—a life with friends, a life with laughter, a life with Anna, and a life with Audrey.

I put her down and she runs over to the dessert table, trying to figure out who made which one. I step into the kitchen to pour another glass of chardonnay. Something trips me and my glass goes flying out of my hand. I try desperately to catch it, but my attempts fail hopelessly. The glass hits the floor, causing a loud, angry crash. Glass flies in all directions. I blink, but when I open my eyes, everything is black. I immediately realize I have gone back to the bad place. Glass continues to shatter around me, even though I know my wineglass has already hit the floor and is no longer breaking.

The angry man is yelling—Benjamin. I can now put a name to this monster. Or at least I think it's him. His voice sounds different from before. "You little shit! Who do you think you are? You think you're tough? Let's see just how tough!" And suddenly, more glass shatters around me, but this time, it hits me. I grab my arm and cry out in pain. The throbbing is uncontrollable. I try to cry, but nothing comes out. I feel the blood gushing from my arm. I squeeze tighter to try to stop it. Suddenly, someone has their arms around my shoulder. "Come on, Julia. Let's get you cleaned up," says the voice. It's a girl. I know her, but at the same time, I don't. She covers me like a blanket, taking me to safety. And then I open my eyes. I'm in the kitchen again. Anna is there now, rubbing my back. "Julia. Julia! Are you okay? Talk to me. What happened?" I look over at her, stunned. I realize now that I confused her voice with the voice in my blackout. There was never a girl there that helped me. It was Anna all along. She had been here the whole time, trying to bring me back. I turn around and see the broken wineglass.

"Anna, I'm so sorry." I gasp, putting my hands to my face in shame.

"Really, Julia, do you think I'm worried about a stupid, broken glass? I'm worried about you. Are you okay?" she asks, holding my shoulders and looking deep into my eyes.

"Yes. I'm fine. Let me help you clean this up."

We work quickly to clean up the mess so no one else notices. Anna sweeps and I squat down to the floor with the dustpan, holding it up just right so that she can brush the shattered pieces perfectly in. It's then—as my arm is outstretched in front of me, holding the dustpan—that I notice something I have never noticed before: a scar on my right arm in the exact same place the glass had cut me in the blackout. It's very subtle but it's there. This just confirms even more that these blackouts are memories that are being triggered. My mind is trying harder than ever to remember what has been forgotten. And it doesn't seem that it's going to stop until it does.

CHAPTER 7

February 14, 2018

I smell roses, champagne, and vanilla-scented candles as I glide slowly down the long hallway. The room I'm approaching is dimly lit. I'm wearing a sleek, silky black dress that shows a little too much of my chest, shoulders, and legs. My hair hangs down long in pretty, effortless curls. I feel beautiful and I must be because when I finally turn the corner and Benjamin turns toward me, his face says it all. He is beaming with happiness as he softly touches my face and pulls me to him. He gently kisses my neck and leads me to a table that is fully set. Two glasses are halfway filled with champagne. Two plates are filled with what looks like a professionally prepared meal. A glass bowl filled with chocolate-covered strawberries takes up the whole center of the table. The soft glow of candlelight surrounds us.

"Happy Valentine's Day, gorgeous," he says as he pulls a chair out and guides me to my seat. I smile and my heart flutters. I pick up my champagne glass and look up at him, but suddenly, his face doesn't look nice anymore. The cleanly shaven skin that was there just moments ago is replaced with rugged stubble and sunken in cheeks. His eyes are now dark and cold and he stares at me with anger. His clothes are ragged and dirty. I look around and realize that the candlelit dinner is also gone. It's replaced with a broken lamp lying on the floor and dirty dishes scattered across the coffee table. The sweet scent of vanilla and roses is replaced with cigarette smoke and garbage. I am no longer wearing a silky black dress. Instead, I'm wearing jeans and a T-shirt and my hair is pulled back in a ponytail.

Suddenly, I start to speak without any warning or control. "What the hell, Benji? I was gone for two days. And I come back and the place is a total wreck! They were here again, weren't they? I told you I didn't want you hanging out with them anymore. You are going to ruin your life! You're going to ruin my life! What has gotten into you?"

His eyes widen and fill with even more rage than before. He comes toward me and shoves me with all his energy. I fall fast and hard directly into the coffee table full of dishes. Plates shatter beneath me. Day-old beer soaks my clothes. My head hits the wooden table as I reach for something to grab, anything. But there's nothing there. The glass digs into my back and immediately starts to throb. I look up to see him coming toward me again, so I cover my face to defend whatever he plans to do next.

He stands over me and shouts fiercely, "Don't you ever come in my house barking orders at me again! I'm a grown-ass man. You better learn your place. Now get up and clean up this mess!"

I sit and uncover my face, but he's gone and so is the coffee table and broken dishes. I'm in a bed. I'm wearing a tank top and sleep shorts. I get up and walk slowly across a bedroom I don't remember seeing before and toward a door that is connected to the room. I turn the knob and push it open, revealing a bathroom. I step in and see him sitting on the floor, hunched over, back against the wall. At first, I think he's sleeping, but then I notice the needle in his arm. I run to him screaming, "Benji! BENJI!"

I fall to my knees and check his pulse. He jumps suddenly at my touch and grabs me by the wrists. I close my eyes and scream. When I open them, he is gone. Now I'm sitting on the floor with my back against the wall. I'm crying, but I don't know why. I'm holding a phone. I look down and see an endless list of calls made to Benji. None of which have been answered. I push myself from the floor to stand up. But something is different. Something feels different. I quickly look down to find an explanation for the strange discomfort in my midsection, but I am not prepared for what I find.

I'm. pregnant.

I wake with a sudden jolt, already screaming—already fighting, kicking, gasping for air. I don't just sit up in bed like usual. This time, I leap from it, landing firmly on my feet. I raise my hands to my head, crying, begging for this to not be true. For the first time since the wreck, the dreams—the memories that have haunted me every single night—have stayed in my mind. And I remember every single second of it. It's a timeline of my past and it's not a pretty one. What a sad life I had. But it's not about me anymore. Where is my child? Is it just as I feared that first night home with Anna? Was my child in that car the night I wrecked? Or is my child with Benji? I'm not sure which is worse. Suddenly, I feel sick. I run to the bathroom but don't make it in time. I can't hold it in anymore. The vomit spews violently from my body, covering my clothes and the floor beneath me. I don't even care. I slide down the wall until I reach the floor and cry hopelessly into the truth that has just been revealed to me.

I cancel dinner plans with Anna and Audrey, claiming that I'm not feeling well. Anna offers to bring me a plate up, but I insist she doesn't come around me in case I'm contagious. Of course, I know I'm not. I'm sick with worry and heartbreak, questions and no answers, fear and disgust. I don't tell her about the dream. I'm still trying to process it myself. For some reason, I feel like I have to deal with this alone for now. I decide to go to the police station the next morning. I pull up Benji's mug shots. I give the date of my wreck. I ask for a list of children that went missing on or around that date. They tell me that people like Benji disappear all the time—that he could be living on the street somewhere, that he could be in a shelter, and that there was a really good chance he could be dead. They tell me that it appears that he had become a full-blown addict, a junkie. Once people get to that state, they lose touch with relatives. People don't hear from them for years at a time. Therefore, even if they were actually missing, in most cases, no one would notice. They also tell me that there were no reports for any missing children in the area around that time. They tell me that they will be on the lookout for anything matching up with the details I have provided, but without any information on my child, they have nothing to look for.

I leave the station feeling even more broken than before. This can't be my fate—to have come so far since the wreck, only to make this horrific discovery and to live the rest of my life never having any answers. I feel completely defeated, consumed with agony and despair. I think back to the dream and the words I spoke to Benji, "You are going to ruin your life. You're going to ruin my life."

And that is exactly what he did. But even worse, he ruined our child's life and possibly even ended it.

CHAPTER 8

April 15, 2018

The last two months have been horrible. I'm not eating. I'm not talking to anyone. I've called into work for the past two weeks straight, claiming to have mono. Anna doesn't even know. She leaves for work every morning, assuming I do the same shortly after. One thing I am doing that I wasn't before is sleeping. In fact, that's pretty much all I've done. I've completely stopped socializing, stopped living. All I do is lay around, sleep, and cry. I've stopped having the dreams altogether now. I guess the last one was too much for my mind and heart to handle, so my body has learned to block them completely. I've shriveled down to nothing. In just two months, I've lost twenty pounds. Some people may think of that as a good thing, but it's not flattering at all. I look like pure death. My eyes are sunken in. My hair is thinning even more than before. My skin is pale, not that I care one bit what I look like right now. It's just what I notice when I happen to pass by a mirror.

I don't remember what it felt like to be a mom, to hold my child. But I do know the second I realized that baby existed, my heart immediately ached for him/her and it hasn't stopped since. I've lost something I didn't even know I had and it is the most gut-wrenching pain I have ever experienced or at least as far as I can remember. But even before, I can't imagine a pain worse than this: to not know if my child is safe, if my child is cold or hungry, if my child is being harmed, or if my child is even still alive. It's something I wouldn't wish on my worst enemy, not even Benji, even though he is the monster that created this hell I'm in. He caused the wreck. I know it. I'm not sure how, but I know he is to blame somehow.

My phone chimes and I unlock the screen, revealing a message from Anna, "Are you okay? I feel like I never see you anymore. Me and Audrey miss you. Please come to dinner tonight. You know you can always talk to me about anything. Whatever it is that you are going through, I can help you through it, Julia. Love you."

I click out of the message. I don't even have the energy to answer. I will eventually, just not right now. Now I just want to sleep. I pull my blanket over my head and wait for unconsciousness to take me away.

I wake suddenly to a knock on my door. I consider not answering it but finally find the energy to peel myself from the sofa. I walk sluggishly to the door and open it slowly. My attention is pulled downward to the sweet, smiling, innocent face of Audrey. "Hi, Juwia! Mom made cookies for you. It's your favorite—peanut butter and chocolate chip. I hope they make you feel better." She holds the plate of cookies up as high as she can toward me and waits patiently for me to accept them. Suddenly, I realize that one of the people I had been avoiding entirely was the one little person that could heal my heart and pull me through this. I was missing a child I couldn't remember, but Audrey was the child that I had loved just like my own since the day that I met her. I grabbed the cookies and set them to the side, then dropped to my knees and wrapped my arms around Audrey, pulling her tightly to me.

"I'm so sorry, Audrey. I'm sorry I haven't been around. I'm sorry I haven't been myself. I'm sorry I haven't been okay." I pull her from me and put my hands on her shoulders. "How about we take these cookies downstairs and eat them together after dinner?" I say, giving the best smile I can.

"Really? You're coming to dinner? Yay!" she cheers.

I smile and tell her to wait while I get my shoes. As I walk away from her, I feel myself crumbling. I quickly wipe away the tears that are rolling down my cheeks. "Get it together, Julia. Do it for Audrey," I whisper under my breath.

I decide to still not mention any of this to Anna at dinner. Even though she can see straight through me and knows I'm not myself, she doesn't push me to give details when I tell her I've just been feeling down.

After dinner, I eat cookies with Audrey as promised, then while she gets ready for bed, I have a glass of wine with Anna. We're mostly silent as we sip our merlot in the cool spring evening on her front porch. She looks at me as if she's looking into my soul. She sees my pain. She sees my brokenness. She opens her mouth to speak but quickly sighs and closes it again. And it's then that I truly look into her eyes and see that she is in pain too. Both of our hearts are screaming to let things out, but neither of our mouths will allow us to do so. I wonder what has caused her pain. I wonder if it could be that she's just worried about me. But I glance at her once again and see something deeper, much deeper. Anna is holding something in just as I am. We know each other so well. We tell each other everything, yet here we are, keeping secrets, allowing ourselves to suffer alone without each other's comfort. Audrey breaks our deepened silence when she comes to the door and says she's ready for bed. She asks if we can both tuck her in so we walk in and place our mostly empty wineglasses in the sink. We tuck her into bed together and say good night. It's not our usual silly, lighthearted good night. It's dark and tortured as if we can't wait to get away from each other, but at the same time, we both long for each other's embrace.

Just as I'm walking out the door, Anna's voice stops me, "Julia, I love you."

I force a smile and tell her I love her too. And just as I turn away and walk out the door, I see a single tear leave her left eye and roll slowly down her cheek.

I'm not sure how we got here. I know what is wrong with me, but I can't imagine what could possibly be wrong with Anna. Maybe Audrey's father had contacted her. Maybe he wanted to come back into her life. But why wouldn't she tell me? Maybe she doesn't want to worry me since I've already been so down. Yes, that's it. Whatever is going on, Anna doesn't want to bother me because she knows I already have something going on. That must be it. I have to start coming around more. The last thing I need is to drift away from my best friend. Maybe I should just tell her what I'm going through. If I do that, maybe she will tell me what's going on with her too. There is no need for either of us suffering alone. I will tell her tomorrow, yes, definitely tomorrow.

I walk upstairs and realize that I no longer want to be alone. After weeks of isolating myself from everything and everyone, the dark emptiness of my apartment now seems to stab at me as I walk through it. The floors seem to creak a little louder. The air seems to feel a little thicker. The eerie sound of the wind howling sends shivers down my spine. I turn every light on and search through TV channels, trying to find something to take my mind to a happier place. I pour another glass of wine and drink it a little faster than I should, desperate to knock the edge off. Finally, I feel myself relaxing as my attention is drawn to a romantic comedy. My eyes get heavier with every single blink and the voices are carried farther away.

"He'll never change, Julia. You have to get out of here," says a familiar voice a few feet away.

I'm sitting at a table, holding an ice pack to my nose. I glance down and see that my shirt is soaked in blood. My own, I'm assuming. I look up to see who is talking to me, but her back is turned and her figure is blurry. I know her voice, but it's so distorted.

"Seriously, Julia, how long are you going to let this go on? What if it's the baby next time? Can you really live with that on your conscience?"

"He just needs help. I love him," I say, sobbing softly through my words.

Suddenly, a baby cries in the distance. My head jerks toward the sound.

"Let me get her. Just keep your nose iced. I'll be right back," says the voice, trailing off toward the baby.

I try to stand, but it's as if my legs are bolted to the chair. I want desperately to get my child. I struggle with every ounce of strength I have, but my body will not budge from the seated position. I start to panic just as I see a shadowed figure approaching me in the hallway. I hear the baby whimpering softly as she comes closer to me. I reach for her, but suddenly, I hit the floor headfirst. I sit up, quickly searching around me. I realize I've fallen off my couch. The romantic comedy blares a cheesy musical number at me as I try to gather myself and stand. My mind struggles to identify the woman—her name, her face. Maybe she was my mother. Could I possibly be remembering someone from my family, someone from my past other than Benji? I close my eyes, digging deep—trying to remember the dream, trying to remember the voice, her tone, her demeanor. And suddenly, I gasp, holding my hands to my chest.

"ANNA!" I scream.

CHAPTER 9

April 16, 2018

"Anna!" I scream frantically, beating on the back door. I know I must look like a maniac. It's 6:00 a.m. and I'm standing here in not nearly enough clothes to be outside. My hair is wild and my voice is shaky. My eyes are swollen from crying. My mind is tormented from over-analyzing. My heart is shattered and searching for answers. "Anna!" I scream so loud my throat feels like I'm swallowing glass. I'm delusional and distraught. I have sat wide awake for the past five hours, forcing myself to wait until daylight to confront her. I didn't want to wake Audrey in the middle of the night. And even now, I don't want to wake her or for her to even see me like this. But I must confront Anna immediately. I can't wait any longer. But she's not answering the door. I'm furious. I know she hears me. I know she's in there!

Until suddenly, I realize she's not. Her car is gone. But why? She never leaves before eight. How did I not hear her car crank? Did she leave early on purpose? Did she know I was coming? Is she hiding from me? My mind is racing. It tries to convince me of things it shouldn't.

I pick up the big gray rock in the flower bed and grab the spare key hidden underneath it. I unlock the door and bust into the house like death itself is chasing me. I search every room, just to be sure no one is there. Once I realize I'm alone, I look around me, suddenly feeling less at home in this house than I ever have before, even my first night here. I look through cabinets and rummage through drawers. I search the hallway closets. Then I find myself in Anna's bedroom. I drop to the floor, pulling everything out from under the bed. I look through her entire dresser, throwing clothes through the air, not caring as they hit the ground. I grab my hair in my fists and scream. The insomnia is starting to collide with the insanity. I'm losing all control of my actions. I briefly consider completely wrecking her whole house, but I reign myself in. I don't know the truth, and it was just a dream. There is no solid proof that Anna knew me before. I need to talk to her now before my mind takes me any further. I run back into the living room to find my phone. I have to call her. We have to talk right now before I go any crazier. I grab it off the counter and start searching for her name in my recent calls. I'm just about to click on it when I glance up for a split second. There in the corner of the kitchen counter is a metal box. I'm not sure how I missed it earlier, but I'm pretty sure I have never seen it there before. I have stood in this kitchen and cooked, talked, and laughed countless times. I have chopped vegetables just inches away from where this metal box now sits. If it was there before, I would have noticed it. I walk slowly toward it, almost as if it is a snake waiting to attack and send its venom running through my veins. Finally, I reach the counter and grab the box, sliding it closer to me. I open it cautiously and carefully, fearing that if I move too quickly, the truth might just jump out and grab me. The first thing I see are my medical records from the accident. I set them to the side, paying them no mind. Next, I see a wedding ring. I have seen it before. It's the engagement ring from the picture of me and Benji. I recognize it almost immediately due to the uniqueness of it. I feel around in the box and quickly find the wedding band that goes with it. I set them on the counter, close my eyes, and take a deep breath. But that doesn't even come close to preparing me for what I find next. It's a photo album and it's one I've never seen before. It's brown leather with tan stitching around the edges. I open it and my heart sinks. My blood boils as if it has suddenly been replaced with flames, burning throughout my entire body. My knees shake and my heart pounds violently. My skin feels as if it is covered in a thousand ants, biting viciously into my flesh. My teeth chatter. My mouth goes dry. I try to swallow, but my throat is like cotton. I stare into the photo, into my own face, as I sit in a hospital bed and gown, holding my baby girl and looking down into her eyes, pure joy beaming from my face. The bottom reads, "Audrey Elayne Harris.

Born on December 17, 2013. Seven pounds. Two ounces. Eighteen inches long."

I stand there for what seems like forever. I'm angry but relieved, heartbroken but overjoyed. My heart races. The feeling of worry and agony in my gut ceases. My baby is alive. My baby is safe. My baby is Audrey. The little girl I have loved all this time is my daughter. I cry tears of joy. But then I think of Anna and rage takes over. My mind doesn't know what to comprehend first: the fact that Audrey is mine or the fact that Anna lied about it.

I find another photo of me holding Audrey. We are sitting outside. I'm wearing a bright summer dress, and she is wearing a onesie of the same colors. The bottom reads, "Julia and Audrey. Six months old."

Next, I find a picture of me on my wedding day, Anna by my side. The bottom simply reads, "Sisters."

How much more can I take? How many more lies are buried? That's all my life is: one big, huge lie. I sob uncontrollably as I flip through more photos of me and Audrey and of me and Anna. And at the very end was an older photo of a woman and two small girls. The writing on the bottom says, "Mama, Anna, and Julia."

I cover my face and gasp for air. The room spins around me. My whole world crashes like bombs being dropped from the sky, exploding and threatening to take me out. And then I hear the doorknob turn. The door opens, and silence and stillness take over. I freeze momentarily before turning to face Anna, my sister, the liar, the traitor. I stand staring at her, my fists clenched at my side. I breathe heavily, angrily. My lips tremble and I think for a second I may actually physically attack her. Her eyes dart back and forth from me to the box. Her mouth drops open. She raises her hands and I see them shaking uncontrollably.

"J-Julia, let—" She starts to cry, and the shaking worsens. "Julia, please, let me explain."

Her body looks as if it is crumbling, as if she will fall to the floor in a million pieces at any second. She grabs onto the door, trying to steady herself.

"Anna, how could you?" My voice is almost unrecognizable to me. I sound like a villain in a movie partly because I'm hoarse from crying last night and screaming for Anna this morning but also because I am so overwhelmed with everything that I have just discovered. My mind, my heart, and my body cannot take anymore.

She holds her hands up in defense and says, "Julia, I know. I know, okay? I know how bad this looks. And it is bad. It's horrible. But please understand. All I have ever tried to do is protect you. You're my baby sister. All I have ever wanted is to keep you safe. Please." She puts her hand to her mouth and closes her eyes tightly, causing more tears to flood out of them. "Please just let me explain."

"Oh, yes, Anna, PLEASE do. Please! Explain why you have lied to me all these years, claiming MY DAUGHTER as your own. Do you want to know what has been wrong with me lately, Anna? I started having dreams about my past. I remembered that I had a child. And I thought she was fucking dead, Anna!" The words hit her like a dagger in her heart. She sobs intensely and falls to the floor. "Where is my daughter? Where is Audrey?" I demand, showing no sympathy to her dramatic display of emotions.

"Julia, wait, please. I will take you to her, but first, you need to hear the whole truth. If you never want to see me or speak to me again, I understand. But you deserve to know everything. Just let me start from the beginning."

CHAPTER 10

September 18, 2004

Anna

It's always so hard to convince myself to come here and then once I do, it's even harder to convince myself to leave. I just want our mama's grave to look nice before winter comes. Once the snow sets in, there will be no hope for any flowers to survive. I trace my fingers over the engravement on the cold tombstone: Elayne Grace Owens. Beloved wife and mother. May 5, 1964–February 27, 2000.

My mother was beautiful. Her dirty-blond hair fell into long ringlets down her back. She had the brightest green eyes and the softest skin. Sweet Julia looks just like her, and thankfully, we both inherited her pure, loving personality. But one quality my mom had was that she was too nice sometimes, too vulnerable, too accepting of others who put her down. I guess that's why she stayed with my stepdad all those years. After my father's death when I was only an infant, I guess she was so heartbroken that she settled for the next man that came along. She let him mistreat her. I see the same trait in Julia and it scares me. We are both like our mother in many ways but that is one trait I did not inherit. I'm a fighter. I stand up for myself and everyone I love. I am willing to do whatever it takes to protect the ones I love no matter what the cost or consequence. I couldn't protect my mother. Her illness was something out of my control. But I was determined I would spend every last breath in my body protecting Julia. I would be turning seventeen in a few months. I was doing everything possible to have myself emancipated and convince the courts I could care for her myself. I had to be careful, though.

Saying just a little too much of the wrong thing could land us in foster care and most likely, we would get separated. I would stop that from happening or die trying. But I knew I had to get us out of that house. My stepdad had always been mean. He always put my mom down, never showed her respect. He never showed any of us love. But since she had died, he had turned into a complete monster. He was basically living off whiskey and cigarettes. He would be gone on drinking binges for days at a time. And when he finally returned, he was even angrier than he was when he left. I wasn't afraid of him, but I was sick of watching my baby sister live in fear. I had to get her out of there before he did any more damage. I could already see the corruption settling in her mind. The words he spoke to her were sticking to her like glue. I knew that if she stayed much longer, she would truly believe that her self-worth was defined by what he told her—that she would truly think that she was pathetic, disgusting, ugly, and worthless. He could say these things to me all day long and they would roll right off my back. I knew the truth was that he was those things, not us. But Julia absorbed it and I could see it becoming her truth with every day that passed. The longer we stayed, the more she believed these things. And the more she believed it, the less chance she had of fighting to prove him wrong. She would end up with a man just like him because she would truly believe that's all she deserved, and I was not going to let that happen. I would not let any man hurt my sister, including her own father.

We place the flowers neatly on our mother's grave and start our walk home. My stepdad has currently been gone for two days and I'm not sure when he will pop back in. So my stomach turns when I hear the radio blaring through the kitchen window as we approach the house. I watch as Julia grips her backpack straps tighter and looks quickly down to the ground, pure terror crossing her face. I put my arm around her shoulder, squeezing tightly. "Hey, don't worry, okay? I got you." I wink at her and smile. She forces a smile back and slightly nods.

We ease into the front door and I tell Julia to head straight to her room. I go into the kitchen to try to scrape up something for dinner so that I can take it to her so she doesn't have to come around him. He's singing loudly along with the music. His words are slurred and he laughs at himself for not being able to keep up with the actual song. He trips and almost falls directly into me right as I'm entering the kitchen. I jump back, and he misses me by an inch. "Move, Anna! You're always in my damn way," he yells, staggering into the living room. I ignore him and search the kitchen to see if any of the food I have hidden is still there. I'm not surprised to find that most of it is gone. Ramen noodles and a peanut butter sandwich will have to do for tonight. I quietly prepare it, making sure not to draw any attention. Soon, I hear him snoring, so I go tell Julia it's safe to come in the kitchen. We eat quietly and do our homework while we have access to the table. Suddenly, the loud rumble of thunder rattles the house without warning.

"He's awake," Julia whispers, looking quickly down at the table.

I lay my hand softly on her arm. "It's okay," I tell her, watching closely to see what his next move is.

He stares us down like a raging bull, snarling as he stumbles toward us. Julia's breathing gets heavier with every step as he approaches us.

"What the hell was that?" he slurs, staring at us.

"It was just thunder," I say calmly, watching his every move. He slams his fist on the table firmly.

"Well, I'm trying to sleep, damn it!" he yells. "And who turned my radio off? I was still listening to that."

"I did," I say, standing from my chair. Julia tries to back me up, but all I need her to do right now is stay quiet.

"We were just trying to get some homework done, Daddy," she says softly.

"Well, I don't give a damn about your homework, you little know-it-alls! Y'all need to quit worrying about all that useless nonsense and get a job anyway. Start doing your part around here!"

And with that, he grabs Julia's notebook and starts ripping pages. The essay that she had worked diligently on for the last three days, weeks of notes taken that she needed for exams, book reports, everything is torn to shreds in seconds. She jumps up, screaming, "No, Daddy, no! Please stop! I need that for class, PLEEEASE!" She sobs hysterically. She reaches up to grab the papers from his grip. I try to stop her, but I'm too late. As she steps toward him, he steps back, trips, and falls straight into the kitchen cabinets. Dishes shatter, falling onto him and crashing into the floor. Glass slices his skin as it continues to fall all around him. I grab Julia and tell her to run, but she is frozen in fear. Her feet might as well be cemented to the floor because she won't budge. I'm not even sure she's breathing. She stands motionless, staring in fear as he fights off chards of glass. When his face finally rises, it's Julia he has in his sights and he is coming for revenge.

"You little shit! Who do you think you are? You think you're tough? Let's see just how tough!" he yells as he starts to throw the broken dishes directly toward her. Half of a broken plate flies straight at her arm, gashing it wide open. I do the only thing I know to do and grab a cast-iron skillet from the top of the stove. I run toward him from the side and swing it toward his head with every bit of strength I have. He doesn't even have time to react. He goes straight to the floor, immediately unconscious. I run to my sister, not knowing how much time we have. "Come on, Julia. Let's get you cleaned up," I say, leading her to the bathroom.

She cringes as I pour peroxide over the wound. I dig desperately through the cabinet until I find Neosporin and bandages. I wrap the bandage securely around her arm and tell her to go pack a bag. "Get whatever you think you can't live without. Leave the rest. We're leaving and we're not coming back. Hurry, Julia!"

I run back into the kitchen, cast-iron skillet raised in the air as precaution. He is still laid out. Should be for a while, but there's no guarantee. I go to my room and stuff as many clothes as I can into a small bag. I grab mom's necklace from my dresser and latch it around my neck. I tell Julia we have to go before he wakes up. We hurry out of the door, just as a heavy rain starts to pour. We make it through the field, out of the gate, and onto the dirt road at the end of the driveway when suddenly, a bolt of lightning illuminates the sky and causes a sharp, loud crack behind us. We look back and see sparks flying from the house as smoke starts to fill the air around it.

"Anna! We have to go back. The house is catching on fire!" Julia screams. "Anna, come on. We have to get him out!" she pleads.

"No, Julia. It's not safe. We're not risking our lives for him. He wouldn't do it for us, and you know it! And how are we going to get him out? If he wakes up, he will just try to hurt us, even if we are trying to save him. Just come on. The rain will put it out. Come on!"

She stands there, staring at our home, rain drenching every inch of her, and sobs. She sobs for a man that never loved her, never loved any of us. She sobs for a man that wasn't worth the air he breathed. She sobs for a man that wouldn't spit on her if she was on fire. She sobs because I won't let her get herself killed trying to pull him out of one. She sobs because she is kindhearted. Even the monster that harms her, she still loves. And she sobs hopelessly and desperately for him. I let her watch and cry for these few seconds, but now it's time to go.

"Come on, Julia! Now!" I demand. She sniffs, wiping a mixture of tears and rain from her face. "You forget he ever existed, Julia. He is not worth a single thought of your precious mind."

We walk for miles without saying a word.

The truth is, I didn't really know if the rain would put that fire out or not. I didn't know how long he would stay unconscious. I didn't know if he would live or die that night. But what I did know was that he would never hurt us again. I told Julia what I had to just so she would leave.

I know she probably thinks I am horrible right now, but I only did what I felt I had to do. I said I would do anything to protect my sister and I meant it.

CHAPTER 11

May 11, 2010

Since I had to drop out of school six years ago so that I could work to support me and Julia, I am over the moon ecstatic that she has managed to stay in school and will be graduating in a week.

I have worked my ass off so that she could succeed and have the life she deserves. Once she's out on her own and able to support herself financially, I plan to go to college myself and pursue a real career. But for now, it's all about Julia. She's smart and responsible. She studies hard. She's levelheaded and mature. She's got her eye on the prize and I know nothing will stop her until she has it. She's been accepted to Duke University with a full scholarship and plans to study biophysics. She is going to kill it. She's not like a lot of other kids that go to college and party and join sororities and have fun. Julia is focused. She's dedicated. She has seen how tough life can be, so she's determined to work hard to make her life good. She's got this. And I could not be more proud of her.

I've been pulling extra shifts waitressing at the diner, and I recently took on a couple of extra houses to clean. I'm hoping to have enough money saved up to buy her a car by this fall. It will have to be a surprise. If she finds out what I'm up to, she will demand I save money for myself. She's always saying I have done too much for her already—that she has to learn to stand on her own two feet. And she will, but first, I have to make sure she has what she needs to get there. She will most likely be hired right out of college, making extremely good money. She can return the favor then. But for now, all I want is to make sure she never has to struggle just to make it like I have—that she never spends hours serving other people food for way too little money, that she never has to be down on her knees scrubbing someone else's toilet, and that she never has to give up her dreams or even has to put them on hold. I just want her to soar. And I know she will. Nothing will get in her way. I just know it.

I text Julia to confirm dinner plans for later and look over my work schedule for next week. I feel exhausted already just thinking about the extra hours. It will all be worth it, though, when Julia is smiling proudly as she drives off to college in her new car. It's so hard to believe that this summer is all we have left together before she moves off to college. I could not be more proud of her, but at the same time, it's hard to let her go. It's always been me and her. We have always had each other. It's so hard to imagine living my life every day without her here with me. Other than our best friend, Gracie, she's all I have. I've never had time to make many friends. I've always been so busy working, trying to support us. And I definitely haven't had time for a relationship. It's always just been me and Julia. Without her, I will be totally alone. I try not to think about it as the sadness flutters in the pit of my stomach.

My phone chimes and distracts me from my sappy thoughts. It's Julia responding to my message, "Yes! See you at six thirty. Love you."

I smile and grab two menus for the people walking in the front door of the diner. It's a guy, maybe a little younger than me, and a girl several years younger.

He seems to come from money and has an arrogance about him that I don't care for. She stares down at the floor, her jacket pulled tightly around her as if she's freezing, even though it's just over 80 degrees outside. *Odd*, I think to myself as I head over to greet them.

"Hi, welcome to Frank's. You can follow me to your seat," I say cheerfully, walking past them.

"Uh, the place is basically empty. I think we can sit wherever we want," the guy says to me, turning in the other direction and guiding the young girl right along with him. She pulls her sleeve tightly around her fist and puts it to her mouth, almost as if she might cry.

"Um, yeah, sure, okay. Sit wherever you like," I say, trying my best not to give him attitude.

The last thing I need right now is to lose my job because I let some prick get the best of me and caused me to go off on him. I set their menus in front of them and ask for their drink orders. The girl stares down at the table, never looking up. "Two waters," the guy says sharply. He waits until I've walked a couple of feet away before he adds, "With lemon," almost as if he's hoping I won't hear him and he can have a reason to complain. But I did hear him, so I turn back and smile as politely as I can manage.

I return with their drinks and ask if they are ready to order. The girl still doesn't look up, and at this point, my stomach is starting to turn. This scenario reminds me far too much of the way my mother was around my father, so I can only imagine what is going on behind closed doors with these two. And this girl is so young. She's barely eighteen if that. I just want to grab her and tell her that she's beautiful, that she's too good to put up with his shit, and that she can do so much better. My heart breaks for her. I try to push all these thoughts to the back of my mind and focus on taking their order. Damn, if I didn't need this job so bad, I would cause a hell of a scene right now.

"We'll both have the BLT with fries," he says, holding up the menus toward me without looking my direction. I glance at her one more time just to see if she shows any response whatsoever for what he just ordered FOR HER. I wonder if while I was away from the table if she actually told him that's what she wanted or if he just decided and she had no say. I can feel my skin starting to burn as I walk to the back to put in the order. I feel my cheeks turn blood red as my heart begins to beat faster and faster. I slam the order down on the counter and turn sharply back around, heading for their table. "Screw this. There's plenty of other restaurants that need waitresses." I'm fully cocked and loaded, ready to unleash my anger at this worthless prick. I bust out of the kitchen full speed with both fists clenched, but suddenly, my mission is pulled right out from under me. They're gone, just two waters with lemon left fully untouched, straws still in the wrappers. I breathe a long, heavy breath and wipe a single tear from my face. Okay, time to get back to work.

"Hi, welcome to Frank's!" I greet the next group of customers walking in the door, quickly scanning the parking lot through the window just to see if they might still be there. Nothing. They're gone. And I guess it's probably better that way. I didn't need to lose my job today.

Later at dinner, I plan to talk to Julia like I have countless times before, reminding her of her self-worth, reminding her that she never has to settle for a man that treats her with anything less than respect and love. I've spent years trying to undo the damage my stepfather did to her, and tonight, I'm shaken up from the couple I saw at the diner earlier. The thought of Julia being with someone like that guy, someone like her father, makes me completely insane. I won't let it happen.

I start my usual pep talk, but Julia interrupts. "Anna, please, can we just not? Please. I get it. I really do. I promise. But I'm a big girl now. I can take care of myself. You don't have to worry about me anymore, okay?" she says, her green eyes beaming brightly at me.

I know she's right. I have to stop mothering her. She's not a little girl anymore. She's becoming a woman. And I have to let her be one.

"Sure," I say, smiling. "I know you can."

CHAPTER 12

November 25, 2011

I have figured out my new normal this past year and a half. I landed a really good job at a law firm as a secretary. I was able to ditch my waitressing and cleaning jobs and move out of the tiny apartment that me and Julia rented before. I bought my first house, a cottage-style home in a great little neighborhood. It's hard without Julia being here, but it's a fresh start since she is fully established in her dorm at Duke. She comes to visit as much as possible and she's heading here now for Thanksgiving break. I am so excited to see her but also curious. She says she wants to talk to me about something. I'm sure it's something good. She is probably doing so great at school that they already have an excellent job lined up for her. Whatever it is, I'm just ready for her to be here.

I'm finishing up some last-minute festive decorating when I hear a car horn blow outside. I open the door and see the black Dodge Charger that I purchased for my baby sister last year, pulling into my driveway. I jump up and down excitedly, and she sticks her head out of the window, screaming and continuing to blow the horn. She barely takes time to throw it into park before she jumps out and we both run to each other, entangling our arms around one another. It's always like this when we first see each other after being away for several months.

We both start grabbing luggage from the trunk and make our way into the house. This will be our first holiday season in my new home, so I've gone out of my way to make it look extra nice.

"Wow, it smells like straight-up November in here, Anna. Did you leave any pumpkin spice candles for the rest of the people?" she jokes, winking at me and throwing her bags on the couch.

"Hey, don't hate on my candles, okay? I think they smell pretty," I return, shoving her gently.

"They do," she says, smiling. "It actually looks really amazing in here. I'm so happy you're doing good enough to get out of that apartment and be somewhere nice like this. You deserve it, Anna."

"Thanks, sis. So what's the big news? I've been dying to know!"

Her expression changes from happy to nervous.

"Um, well," she says, biting her lip, "there's actually someone I want you to meet."

"Oh! Do you have friends coming from school? Is it your roommate? I've been wanting to meet her for so long! I have an extra room if she wants to stay!" I say, getting ahead of myself.

"Actually, Anna, it's a guy."

"Oh." My expression falls flat. I'm not at all ready for this. I just assumed she would stay single while in college to stay focused on her grades. A guy will just distract her. Okay, here I go, mothering again. She's a big girl, Anna. Get yourself together. "Um, okay. Is he from your school? Do you have classes together?"

She sits straighter and crosses her hands in her lap. "No, no, he doesn't go to my school. He actually lives here in town. I met him while I was home over the summer. We stayed in touch, and he's been up to visit me a few times. I really like him, Anna. I hope you will too. I was hoping maybe he could come for dinner tonight. I mean if it's not too much trouble. I can help you cook. I just really want you to meet him and I'm kind of excited to see him now that I'm in town."

The reality hits me a little harder than I'm prepared for. I really thought that I was the only person Julia was rushing home to see, but all this time, there has been this guy that I knew nothing about that she has been giddy and excited to be with. I would be lying if I said I didn't feel a little crushed right now, but I do my best not to let her see.

"Yes, of course he can. Um, just tell him to be here around five."

"Thanks! You're the best!" She squeals, jumping up and hugging me.

I pour my third glass of wine and pull the ceramic baking dish filled with chicken and vegetables from the oven. It's four forty-five and I'm a ball of nerves. I'm trying to be upbeat and appear to be just as excited to meet this guy as Julia is for me to, but I'm honestly just dreading it and want it to be over. I was so excited to spend this week with her and now I have a feeling I will barely even see her. She will most likely be spending every second possible with Mr. Right the whole time she is here.

The doorbell rings and my stomach turns. I grab my wineglass and suck down half of its contents before following behind Julia as she trots happily to the door. I stand back and watch as she opens it, and they embrace each other and fall into a long intimate kiss that makes me feel as if I'm going to be sick. She pulls away from him slowly and grabs his hand, leading him into the house. I see that he is handsome and dressed nice. But there is something else about him that I can't quite put my finger on. It's not until he speaks that it hits me like a thousand bricks crashing into my chest.

"Hi, I'm Benji," he says, holding his hand out to shake mine.

But instead of my hand greeting his, it flies up to my face to cover my mouth. I press it firmly, trying to stop the vomit that threatens to leave it. I back away slowly as my skin starts to tingle. His hair is longer and he's more muscular than before. But he still has that cocky smile and his kind eyes don't fool me for one second. I try hard to fight it, to deny the reality that surrounds me, the truth that stands right before me.

My sister is dating the guy from the diner that I waited on last year, the guy that had his girlfriend too scared to speak or even look up, the guy that wouldn't even let her order her own food, the guy that treated me like pure shit from the second he walked in the door. He has no idea who I am. He doesn't remember me because I was just someone else he walked right over. But I remember him. And now my worst fear has come true. My sister has fallen for a loser, an abuser, a monster. I try to contain my anger, but it burst out of me like flames from a furnace.

"Get out! Get out of my house and stay the hell away from my sister!" I yell violently.

"Whoa," he says, raising his hands in defense and backing away slowly.

"Anna, what the hell? What are you doing?" Julia screams.

"Julia, you don't really know this guy. You don't know the way he treats girls. He has to leave now! And you need to stay away from him."

I cross my arms, waiting for her to tell him to leave, but she doesn't.

"Anna, you're being crazy. How are you going to tell me I don't know him when I've known him for months and you literally just met him?"

She's not hearing me. Does she really think I would say this if it weren't true?

"Julia, I saw him in the diner one day last year. He was with this girl and she just seemed so—"

"Anna, really? You saw him in the diner one day and so you think you know him better than me? You don't know anything about him. Honestly, I can't even be around you right now. If he's leaving, then I am going with him. I really hope you snap out of it before I come back."

And with that, she grabs his arm and they storm out of the door.

Julia has never talked to me like that. She's never turned on me.

I mean I admit my reaction was a little dramatic, but it's only because I wanted to protect her. Surely, she will see that. But what if she doesn't? What if I really have to accept that she and this jerk are a couple? Chills cover my body as the thought taunts my mind. I sit quietly at the table, staring at the meal that I just spent over an hour preparing that will now not be eaten.

November 26, 2012

I send a text to Julia, "Julia, can we please talk? I'm sorry I over-reacted. Please, just call me."

I sit numbly, staring at my phone, waiting for a response. I've done a lot of thinking since last night. Really, I've thought all night long. I sat up almost the entire night stressing, worrying, crying, thinking. If my sister has fallen for this boy, I have to make peace with it. If not, I will lose her. She had that crazy look in her eye, like she's in love, and she will do anything to prove it. I cannot let this guy be my enemy if he has my sister's heart. I have to apologize for the way I acted, even if I know he is a total jerk not worthy of a single second of my baby sister's attention. I will play nice for now. But the second I see that he has hurt her, I will rip him to shreds.

Finally, the chime of my phone reassures me I haven't lost her.

Julia replies, "Yeah, okay. Let's talk. But you have to be nicer to Benji or I'm out."

I sigh a long breath of relief. I wasn't sure she would answer me. We make plans to meet for lunch, just the two of us.

As I'm sitting at the table in a local bistro waiting, something catches my eye. Or someone, I should say. She's walking confidently through the door. She wears a long coat and sunglasses. Her hair and makeup is done just right. She waves casually and speaks politely to people as she passes by. She's beautiful. She's flawless. And suddenly, I realize my baby sister is no longer a baby. She's no longer a child. Julia is now a woman and it shines through her brighter than the sun. I shift in my seat nervously as she sits across from me and crosses her hands on the table.

"So what exactly is it that you would like to talk about, Anna?" she says, raising one eyebrow as if we are playing a game of poker.

"Um, I just want to say I'm sorry, Julia. I'm sorry I was rude to your friend. I'm sorry I judged him after only one brief encounter. I'm sorry I ruined our night."

I swallow hard as the words burn in my throat and threaten to violently come back up and splatter on top of the perfectly set table we are seated at.

My stomach turns as I watch her expression. I watch at how dismissive she is of me. After everything I have done for her, she is choosing this piece of shit scum of the earth loser over me. But it's okay. I will continue to do whatever it takes to make sure she is okay, to make sure she is successful, and to make sure she is safe. I'm watching you, Benji. I'm watching and waiting. And the second you slip up, the very second you hurt my sister, I will be here waiting. I will be who she runs to, and you will no longer be existent in her world, in our world. You will be gone, just as quick as you came. You will not hurt my sister, you or anyone else.

I will make sure of it.

CHAPTER 13

November 28, 2011

Here I am in the kitchen, once again nervously awaiting Benji's arrival. But this time, I'm fully aware of who I'm waiting on. This time, I am preparing myself to pretend to be sorry, to pretend to like him, to pretend that I am the one that was wrong—all so Julia doesn't hate me and we can hopefully still have a pleasant Thanksgiving holiday together. I'm snapping the ends off the asparagus, trying to get all the prep work done ahead of time for tomorrow's big meal when I hear the doorbell ring. Maybe it's just me, but it sounds a little louder now than it ever has before—angrier, like it's yelling at me rather than notifying me of someone's arrival. Julia stops setting the table and looks me dead in my eyes as if to warn me to be on my best behavior. She places the stack of dinner plates on the table and walks slowly to the door. I don't follow her this time.

After a couple of minutes, she walks back into the kitchen, Benji trailing behind her. His hands are in his coat pockets, shoulders hunched up, as he creeps slowly toward me, careful not to wake the beast within me that is ready to attack at any moment. I set the remaining asparagus in the colander and wipe my hands quickly on my apron.

I take a couple of steps toward him and force a smile, which I'm sure comes out looking anything but happy, but it's the best I can do right now.

"Hi, Benji. I would just like to say that I'm sorry. I don't know you and I shouldn't have judged you the way I did. I'm just very protective of my little sister and I don't want her getting hurt. I hope that you will be able to join us for dinner tomorrow and we can have a fresh start."

Julia nods her head in approval as I speak and quickly darts her eyes toward him as she waits for his reaction.

"Thanks, I appreciate that. But I have dinner plans with my family already. Apology accepted, though. We're good."

He holds his hand out toward me and I force myself to shake it. He then puts his arm around Julia and kisses her forehead. I turn and walk back to my asparagus. My job here is done. No need to continue to make myself talk to this jackass or stand one single inch closer to him than I have to. He asks Julia if she needs any help before he heads out, and she tells him he can help her finish setting the table. I cringe as I watch him grab my brand-new set of dishes. To be honest, I don't want him touching them. I don't want him touching anything that belongs to me. And I don't want him touching my sister. But I bite my tongue, careful not to get in trouble with Julia again. Thankfully, once they finish with the table, he says he has to go. I say a quick goodbye before Julia walks him to the door and then take a deep sigh of relief. I hope that this is the last time I see him while she's here visiting. Honestly, I hope it's the last time I see him ever, but I have a very strong feeling it won't be.

Soon, Julia returns to the kitchen and quietly moves to the next thing on our to-do list. She doesn't look at me. She doesn't speak to me. I've apologized to Benji, but deep down inside, she's still angry for the way I acted and I really can't blame her. I quickly try to think of a way to lighten the mood, anything to put a smile back on her face and get us laughing and cutting up like we always do.

"Hey! I have an idea." She cuts her eyes at me, waiting to shoot down whatever it is I'm about to say. "Let's both make a dessert for dinner tomorrow. I have tons of baking items in my pantry. We won't tell each other what we're making, and at dinner, we won't tell anybody who made what. After everyone has tasted it, we will get them to vote on which one is best and see who wins. Just a little friendly competition. Whatcha say?"

She grins slyly and crosses her arms.

"You're on."

We both run to the counter and start grabbing recipe books. We playfully push each other, and she grabs a book right out of my hand and runs off with it. I snatch it back from her right as she's making her escape. She screams, and suddenly, we are both frantically searching for dessert recipes, laughing hysterically as we try to throw each other off course.

It worked. She's back. We're back. And now that Benji is gone for the night and has plans for tomorrow, I have my sister to myself for Thanksgiving. It will be like always, just us, friends and family. No Benji. And just that alone is enough to be thankful for.

CHAPTER 14

June 5, 2012

I've been sitting here, waiting for at least an hour. I hate airports. I hate the smell. I hate the rush of crowded people. I'm not a traveler. I like the security of my own home. But Julia insisted that we take a beach trip, just the two of us, and since I hardly ever get to see her anymore, I couldn't possibly say no.

Finally, I see her in the distance, waving excitedly and rushing toward me, dragging her luggage behind her. I jump up and run to greet her.

"We have to hurry or we'll miss our flight. I was starting to think you stood me up!"

I jokingly shove her to the side and start grabbing my bags from the seat next to where I was sitting.

"I know. I know. I'm sorry. I had car trouble. I had to get my roommate to give me a ride."

We run as quickly as we can, luggage in tow, until we finally make it to our line to board the plane. This will be the first time either of us have been to the beach. I must admit. I am pretty excited to sit back with my toes in the sand and listen to the peaceful sound of waves crashing. It's just the flight that stresses me out. But it will be all worth it once we get there. I am determined I won't let anything ruin this trip for me.

Once we are on the plane, we order a glass of wine and fill each other in on what's been going on in our lives. We giggle like two children at the older man snoring behind us. I tell Julia how I've become a part of my neighborhood and made friends with everyone. She tells me about her fun nights out on the town with her group of friends from school. And then she starts talking about Benji. Suddenly, there is a twinkle in her eyes that wasn't there before his name left her lips. She is obviously trying to stop herself from smiling but can't. She's giddy over this guy and I just can't see why. I mean, I have seen them together a couple of times since Thanksgiving and I guess things seemed okay. I've never seen him act mean or disrespectful. And she's never shown signs of being mistreated. But there is just a twisting feeling in my gut every time she mentions his name. I just can't shake it. I have the worst feeling about this guy and I can't move past it. I honestly don't know what it is that she sees in him, but it's quite obvious at this point. She is head over heels in love. I'm trying to make the best of it, but at the same time, I wish he would just disappear. She could do so much better than him.

Once we arrive at the condo, we immediately change into our swimsuits and head out to the beach. We're both exhausted from the flight but also can't wait to get our toes in the sand. The sun is starting to set and there's a nice breeze blowing, so it's not miserably hot at the moment. We sit back in our chairs and just take a second to breathe it all in.

But suddenly, Julia breaks the silence, right along with my heart, sanity, and peace of mind.

"So I have some news."

She turns toward me, her lips pursed tightly together, almost as if she might burst if she doesn't let her secret out.

She doesn't give me time to respond, and before I know it, she's flashing a diamond ring in my face and squealing.

"I'm engaged!"

My heart sinks. I fight with every ounce of strength I have to look happy, to show even the slightest bit of excitement for her. I know she needs that from me. I know that I am the one person she was probably most anxious and excited to deliver this news to. But happy is the farthest from what I'm feeling right now. If I'm being honest, it's everything I can do not to puke all over this pretty white sand. It's all I can do not to snatch that sparkling diamond off her finger and throw it straight into the angry crashing waves just a few feet away from us. It's all I can do not to burst into tears. I roll all these feelings into one huge ball and try to swallow them down and not act on any of them. My mouth hangs open as I stare at her in shock and disbelief.

"I know. It's unexpected. And I know it's really fast. We've only been dating a few months blah, blah, blah. I know what you're going to say, Anna. But I love him. I really do. And I'm REALLY happy. So if you could just be happy for me, that would be great." She stares down at the ring, smiling hopelessly, and then looks up at me to see my response.

"Um, congratulations. I'm really happy for you, Julia."

She squeals again and throws herself toward me, wrapping her arms around my shoulders and squeezing tightly. I squeeze her back and quickly reach up and wipe the flow of tears from my face before she sees them.

She pulls back and grabs my shoulders.

"So, yeah. That's why I wanted you to come on this trip with me. This is kind of my bachelorette trip!"

"Wait. What? No, Julia, you do that right before the wedding. I mean, you're going to wait until you're finished with school to actually get married, right?" I stare into her eyes, desperately waiting for her answer, waiting for her to calm my anxious, beating heart.

"We're getting married next month! The truth is, Anna, I've been engaged since February—Valentine's Day to be exact. I have just been too afraid to tell you. Benji surprised me with the sweetest romantic dinner that he made himself. He had scented candles, chocolate-covered strawberries, all that. And at the end of dinner, he proposed. I was so excited. The first person I wanted to tell was you. But I was afraid you wouldn't be excited for me. The thing is, Anna, I'm going to put school on hold for now. His parents have money, like real money, the kind of money we don't know anything about. He says they could help me get any job I want. They know people. They have connections everywhere. And Benji even says I don't have to work. He makes plenty of money. He doesn't want me to feel obligated to have a job. He says I can be a stay-at-home mom if I want!"

She looks up into the sky as if she's daydreaming.

"Mom? Julia! Are you pregnant?" Now I'm sure I'm going to be sick. I grab my stomach, terrified of what her answer will be.

"No, Anna. Chill out! I'm just talking about one day in the future. I'm sure we'll have kids eventually."

"Julia, are you serious right now? After everything I've done for you. I literally put my own life on hold and worked my ass off so that you could have a good education—so that you could be successful. And now you're just going to throw it all away on some guy you've only known a few months. You need to be financially stable on your own first, not depending on some guy you barely know to fully support you!" I scream frantically.

Her expression changes and she jumps up. "Yes, Anna, I know you worked hard. I know you wanted me to have a good education and I am grateful for that. But I never asked you to do any of that. You can't use what you did for me to control my life. I'm not a kid anymore. I'm a grown woman. You have to let me make my own decisions, Anna! I knew you would do this. I knew you wouldn't just be happy for me! You are not my mother! Why can't you just be my sister for once and not freak out?"

She bursts into tears and runs off toward the condo before I can even respond. I start to get up and go after her, but when I try to, I feel like every single bit of life and energy has just been sucked from my body. All I can do is sit and cry. I'm losing the only person I have left. Everything I have done has been for nothing. Benji has won. He is taking her from me and there is nothing I can do.

CHAPTER 15

July 17, 2012

Today, my little sister walks down the aisle and I have a feeling this will be the day that changes our lives forever. She is fully convinced that this is the beginning of happily ever after, but I know better.

I'm trying to pull myself together, trying to bury my anxiety and cover the worry on my face, the ache in my chest, the twisting knot in my stomach. I have done everything in my power to try to talk her out of this for the past month, but Julia has made it very clear that she is going to marry Benji whether I like it or not and I can see that she won't back down. I have realized that I have no choice but to accept it and hope for the best. I would really love to be wrong about this, about him, about them. I would love for them to have a beautiful life together that resulted in her smiling every day. But I feel certain that I am right. Benji is no good. I just know it. He is going to try to isolate her. He is going to try to push me completely out of the picture. He is going to try to make her believe that he is the only person that she needs in her life. And my biggest fear—the fear that keeps me up at night, tossing and turning and gasping for air because I feel like all of it has been sucked from my lungs—is that she will let him.

I tap softly on the dressing room door, my bridesmaid dress draped over my arm and makeup bag in hand. The wedding planner opens the door just wide enough for me to slip in. Benji's parents have gone completely overboard paying for this wedding. They are probably just thankful that someone actually loves their poor excuse of a son enough to marry him.

I walk in slowly, searching for Julia, and then I see her, standing with her back to me. She's on the other side of the room, talking and laughing with the other bridesmaids. Her long white dress trails far behind her. Her skin is golden brown and her hair is done in the most elegant style. I can't even see her face and still, she takes my breath away. And then she turns toward me and I know immediately that she is the most beautiful bride I have ever seen. Her face lights up and she runs toward me, holding her dress up, careful not to trip. I put my game face on and fake a smile as we wrap our arms around each other. The last thing I want to do is ruin her special day for her, even if it is ripping my heart right out of my chest.

"Come on! Miranda will get started on your makeup!" She grabs my hand and pulls me over to a line of chairs, where some of the other bridesmaids are getting their hair and makeup done. I'm introduced to her roommate and other friends from school. I'm offered chocolate-covered strawberries and white wine from the caterer. I have never even heard of having the caterers in the dressing room but whatever. I think it's ridiculous, but that doesn't mean I'm going to turn it down. I hear the door open and turn to see who it is and I'm thankful when I see Gracie walk into the room. I've always been Julia's rock, but Gracie has always been mine. She was there for both of us through all the years we struggled. She was there for us when our mom died. She was there through the harsh years we dealt with my stepdad afterward. She was there when we left our home and stepped out into the world alone. She was always there. She's almost like our third sister. Julia and I both think the world of her. Our eyes meet as soon as she looks in my direction. She shares my concerns about this marriage and she's helped me through this as much as possible. She walks over to me before she even tries to find Julia.

"How are you holding up?" She puts her hand on my shoulder and squeezes softly.

"Well, there's chocolate-covered strawberries so, you know, all is well."

I roll my eyes and we both start to laugh, but then I start to cry. She hugs me quickly and then whispers in my ear, "Okay, now get it together. Here she comes." She greets Julia excitedly and I turn around and do just that. I get it together before Julia sees me. Damn, this is going to be a long day.

Later, at the reception, I notice Benji's parents standing in a corner away from everyone. The expressions on their faces are solemn, cold, emotionless, not the faces of parents who just attended their son's wedding. I have never really gotten the chance to properly meet them, so I make my way over to where they are standing so I can try to get to know them a little and just see if they are anything like Benji.

"Hi, um, I'm Anna. We met briefly at the rehearsal dinner. I'm Julia's older sister." I stand with my hand out for what seems like eternity before they finally shake it and acknowledge my presence. I immediately regret my decision to walk over to them. I'm already attempting to escape when Benji's mother stops me.

"So, big sister. Anna, is it? How do you feel about this marriage?"

My throat starts to close. I was not expecting to be interrogated. And this woman is literally one of the most intimidating people I have ever met. I might just pee my pants right here in this room full of people. The cold, hard stare she is giving me sends chills running down my spine.

"Um, well, I mean… I feel like…you know. Honestly, I think it's a little soon." My eyes widen as I await her response. I feel as if she may start spitting bullets at me at any second.

"Hmm, is that so?" She crosses her hands in front of her. "I couldn't agree more."

She glares fiercely off into the distance. I look back to see who she's looking at and I realize she's looking straight at Benji and Julia. And then it hits me. She hates Julia. She thinks she's after his money. She thinks that we are trash. I can see it all over her rich, snobby face. She thinks my sister—my perfect, innocent, sweet, beautiful Julia— is not good enough for Benji! As if things weren't bad enough already. I immediately wonder if she has acted this way right to Julia's face or if she has put on an act and pretended to like her. I feel my face turning red. Suddenly, I'm not so intimidated by this woman anymore. In fact, I'm pissed at her. I want to scream at her and tell her how much better my sister can do than her pathetic, loser son. But then all those thoughts come crashing down when she speaks again.

"She seems like a sweet girl. I just hope he doesn't take her down with him." And with that, she turns and walks away. Suddenly, I can't swallow. I feel like the room is spinning. All the dancing figures around me turn blurry. I reach to grab onto something to keep from falling, but there is nothing there. The anxiety I have been trying to bury deep inside of me all day is fighting its way out of me. I just might faint. But then someone grabs my arm and helps me over to the wall. I feel the sweat starting to puddle on my face. I look up and see Benji's dad staring down at me, smiling.

"You ok? You look a little pale. My wife is not as scary as she seems. In fact, she used to be a hell of a lot of fun. I guess Benji sucked every bit of it out of her. He's been a handful—that one. I just hope your sister can turn him around once and for all."

"Uh, I… What did she mean—take her down with him? And what do you mean? What has he done?" I suddenly feel like I'm standing in a furnace. I wipe my face and fan it with my hand, trying to cool down, not caring one bit if I just smeared half of my makeup off.

"Drugs, all of them. We've paid thousands on rehab. He's gone once a year for the past three years. It always seems to be the same thing. He gets clean. He's doing great for a few months. He finds a sweet young girl, full of life, and before you know it, she's not so full of life anymore. He really does seem to love your sister, though. I hope the best for them. Hope she can turn him around. I really do hope so because this is his last chance. We've paid for the rehab. We've paid his bail. And now we've paid for this wedding. If he slips again, we're done with him. I'm sorry. I've probably said too much. You try to have a good night."

He nods his head and walks off to find his wife. I stand there against that wall. The dagger in my heart twists and salt pours on my wound. Even his own parents see it. Even his parents are concerned for Julia. I walk weakly toward the restroom, barely able to stand, fully depending on this wall to help me along the way. I make it to the sink and splash water on my face. My reflection in the mirror triples and blurs. I grab onto the counter for support. I feel my arms going numb and I know that I have to pull through this. I close my eyes and breathe deeply. And it's in that moment that God proves once more to be real because Gracie, of all people, walks into the restroom. She comes running to me when she sees my condition. When I realize it's her, I know it's safe to lose it. I let it all out, and she's there to catch me once again. She locks the door so no one else can come in and she holds me while I cry, coaching me through breathing exercises, allowing me to fall apart, while at the same time putting me back together.

By the time we make it out of the bathroom, Julia and Benji are leaving. I want desperately to run to her, to tell her not to go, to tell her what I've found out. But I've already learned that telling her these things gets me nowhere. If I'm going to protect her, I have to keep my mouth shut from now on. I have to make sure that I don't do anything that makes her mad, or gives her any reason to push me away. I have to make sure that I'm there. So when he messes up, she runs to me.

I hug her goodbye, and she questions why I'm sweating, why my hair and makeup are messed up, why my eyes are puffy and red. I lie and say I have been sick to my stomach. She believes me and wishes me well, hugging me one last time. She runs off and grabs Benji's arm and he escorts her to the car. He opens the door and she hops in and waves excitedly at everyone. They pull off and I force a smile once again and wave as the words *just married* fade away into the distance and I watch my little sister drive away with a monster.

CHAPTER 16

October 6, 2012

I wave and smile excitedly as I see Julia approaching the table I'm seated at in a small café downtown. She gives what looks like a very forced smile and slightly throws her hand up to return my wave. She has worry, stress, and fear written all over her face. I can see already that she's trying to hide it, but I could already tell something was wrong over the phone simply by the tone in her voice. I also thought it was strange for her to randomly insist on coming to stay with me for a couple of days when her and Benji are still practically newly-weds. I mean, don't get me wrong, I cherish every second I can get with her these days. It's just really surprising that she had this sudden urge to get away from him.

I stand up and hug her, but this hug is different from our usual greeting. She doesn't squeal in excitement to see me. She doesn't laugh and joke around. She just wraps her arms around me tightly and stands there, squeezing me as if she's afraid that I may disappear if she lets go. I hug her back and fight back tears. I just want to scream. I just want to know what he has done to her to bring her to this point. But I have to play my cards right and be patient or she won't tell me anything. I try my best to act casual and unsuspecting as she releases me and we take our seats.

"So how is married life?" I clear my throat and run my finger along the rim of my coffee mug as my eyes dart nervously around the room.

"Um, it's not what I expected. It's hard. I don't know. Maybe." She pauses and turns her head away for a few seconds. When she turns to face me again, I see that her eyes are full of tears. "Maybe you were right, Anna. Maybe I should have waited."

Exactly what I didn't want—to be right. Yet here we are. I won't dare say I told you so, but I did in fact tell her so, begged her even. But I guess when you are young and in love, you see things differently. You have a different kind of hope in your heart that blinds you to reality.

"I'm so sorry, Julia. What happened?"

She wipes a tear from each cheek and tries hard to hold in any more that threaten to fall.

"I don't know, Anna. He's different. He's changed. He is not the man he was a few months ago. I swear he treated me like a queen before and now I feel like he treats me like his doormat. And he's been hanging out with these people lately. He says they're old friends that he just got back in touch with. They really creep me out. There's something off about them. And I really started noticing him change once they started coming around. I told him I didn't want them in our apartment anymore, but I honestly don't know if he will listen or not. He seems so angry all the time." She starts to sob uncontrollably despite her desperate attempts not to.

I have literally never felt as helpless as I feel right now. I knew it. I knew this would happen. I knew he would hurt her. I try to pull myself together for Julia's sake, but I can feel my cheeks burning like embers from a fire on a cold winter's night. I think back to that day in the diner when I first saw Benji. I remember the look that poor girl had on her face the entire time they were in there. And now as I sit across the table from my little sister all these years later, she, too, wears the same expression. The anger boils inside me, my palms start to sweat, and my throat starts to close up. I close my eyes and tell myself that I cannot lose it right now. Julia needs me.

I open my eyes, reach across the table, and grab her hand.

"Julia, you need to leave him now before things get worse."

She covers her face and continues to sob. "I can't, Anna. I love him. And we're not just dating. We're married. I have to fight for this. I have to try to make it work." My heart shatters even more at her response, but I honestly can't say I'm surprised. That would have been far too easy.

I try to spend her entire visit distracting her and just having fun like we used to. I take her shopping, we stay up late watching movies, we cook together, she helps me decorate for Halloween, but even when she's smiling, she never looks fully happy. When it's time for her to leave, I beg her to stay longer. And when she doesn't, I sit on the couch, crying for at least an hour after she leaves. I'm so afraid for her, so worried. And yet there is nothing I can do. Things will only get worse, much worse. I know it and I am not really sure what level of crazy is going to be released from me when it does.

I wake to a sudden hard knock on the door and jump straight up. I realize I have literally cried myself to sleep on the couch. I rush to the door, expecting to find a neighbor on the other side of it, but instead, I find Julia. She's crying hysterically. Her clothes are soiled and reek of alcohol and I'm not sure what else. Then I notice that her sweater is torn and stained with blood. Her faced is streamed with black from her running mascara. I feel as if someone has just thrown a huge rock at my chest as I stand there frozen. I want to grab her and pull her to me, but she is obviously injured, so I'm afraid I will hurt her worse.

"Julia, what the hell did he do to you?"

She lets out a long, angry cry and runs to me. I lead her over to the couch and sit her down beside me. All I can do right now is hold her. She crumbles into a million pieces in my arms as she lets it all out. She's crying so hard I can barely understand her.

"He pushed me. I hit my head. My back is all cut up. Those people were there while I was gone. The house was a wreck. He looked like a monster. I hate him."

"Julia, you have to call the police. You HAVE TO FILE A REPORT." I hold her shoulders tightly and look her firmly in her eyes.

"No, Anna, please. Just leave it alone. Please. I just want to get cleaned up and go to sleep. Please don't argue with me."

And it's that very moment that I know. I know that in a day or two, she will be driving straight back to him. I know that this is the first of many nights like tonight. I know that she will never leave him no matter what. And I am absolutely terrified of what the outcome will be.

CHAPTER 17

December 31, 2012

Julia

Benji has convinced me to have a bonfire tonight to celebrate New Year's. But really, all I want to do is crawl in a hole and hide from him, from his addict friends, from my stupid mistake of marrying him, from my whole life. I feel so pathetic, so naive. Anna tried to tell me and I just wouldn't listen. Now here I am, only twenty years old, married to a man who has become a monster, married to a man that I am afraid of, married to a man that I'm pretty sure never really loved me in the first place. I've ruined my chance at a good education all for him and now I'm stuck. I've ruined my life. All I want is to run to Anna and cry. But I got myself into this. I wanted to be grown, and so now I have to be a big girl. I have to try to make this work. I have to fight. The only thing worse than being twenty and married is being twenty and divorced.

I slip on my jacket and boots and head outside to join everyone at the fire. Benji is already more than halfway through a pint of Jack and it doesn't look like he's slowing down any. I walk over and take a seat as far away from everyone as possible. One of Benji's friend's girlfriend makes her way toward me and I grit my teeth the whole time she approaches me. She also appears to be wasted but she's only drinking water, so who knows what she's actually on.

"Hey, Julia! Great party." She leans sideways and flares her arms out into the air as if she thinks she can fly.

"Hi, Renee."

I keep my tone as cold and dry as possible and look away as I respond to her, stuffing my hands in my jacket pocket, hoping she will get the message and just leave me alone. Of course, she doesn't. Instead, she grabs a chair and pulls it as physically close to me as she possibly can and sits down. If she were sitting any closer, she would be in my lap. I continue to look away and show disinterest, but she will not take a hint. She goes on and on and on about a new club she went to last weekend and about her upcoming birthday trip to Cabo. Finally, I reach my breaking point. I literally cannot sit here and listen to her anymore. Besides, half of what she's saying is not even making any sense.

"Renee, could you just…could you just shut the hell up already? I really just want to be left alone, okay?"

I stand up and walk toward the house, and she sits, giggling. "WELL, EXCUSE ME!"

I roll my eyes at the fact that she still doesn't get it. The radio is blaring and playing some stupid song I can't stand. Someone starts to shoot fireworks just a few feet away. It's starting to make my head pound. I just want to disappear.

And that's exactly what I'm about to do. But suddenly, out of nowhere, Benji grabs my arm. He squeezes tightly and looks at me with all the rage in the world.

"You're hurting me." I pull my arm, but he only squeezes tighter.

"Dammit, Julia! Why do you always have to ruin everything? Why can't you just calm down and have fun for a change?"

Apparently, he saw me snap on Renee, and rather than ask me what's wrong, he is going to defend her and turn on me. Seriously, husband of the year right here.

I try again to free my arm. I just want to get away from here. "Let me go. PLEASE." I start to get desperate as his grip continues to tighten. Panic sets in, and I start struggling violently. Fireworks continue to shoot all around us. The music continues to blare over the radio. Everyone goes on about their business. No one tries to help me. I continue to struggle frantically, and suddenly, Benji pushes me with all his might. I struggle to catch myself, but I'm caught off guard. The ground greets me with a harsh blow to my entire body and knocks the breath out of me as I cry out in pain. I roll over, gasping for air and struggling to push myself off the ground. I look up to see if he's coming for me again. But he's just standing there, staring at me. "Don't ever embarrass me in front of my friends again, Julia."

He walks back over to the crowd and continues talking and laughing like nothing ever happened. Rage runs through my veins like a wildfire. I do not deserve this. I took enough crap from my dad. I am not going to take it from my husband too. If I want him to learn a lesson, then I have to teach him one. I have to show him that this abuse will not be tolerated. I slowly pick myself up off the ground and walk into the house. I walk into the bedroom and shut the door. I pick up my phone and start dialing.

"911. What's your emergency?"

"I need to report a case of domestic violence, please."

January 1, 2013

The smell of coffee and cinnamon rolls fills the air around me. I smile and roll over slowly but quickly stop myself when the soreness from last night's fall catches me off guard. I open my eyes and feel the safety of Anna's cozy cottage embracing me. I just wish I could feel this safe forever. I sit up and see Anna sitting at the table, sipping coffee. I called her immediately after my call to the cops last night. She arrived shortly after they did and brought me back home with her. I remember the look on Benji's face as the cops cuffed him and read him his rights. I remember the look of shock that he gave me as they stuffed him into the back of that patrol car. I stood on the steps, arms crossed, with my best poker face on. I wanted him to understand that was the last time he put his hands on me.

I stand up, walk over to the table, and sit down by Anna. She gets up without saying a word and walks over to the coffeepot to pour me a cup. She walks back over and sits it, and a plate of cinnamon rolls in front of me on the table.

She looks angry and exhausted.

"Julia, please. Please tell me you are going to leave him this time. Please."

I sigh and pick up my coffee cup. "I don't know yet."

She puts her elbows on the table and cradles her forehead in her palms. I can feel the disappointment radiating off her like a heat wave. I know she thinks I'm ridiculous. I know she doesn't understand why I would ever give him another chance. But she's never actually been in a real relationship, so she wouldn't get it. When you truly love someone, you fight for them, even if you get hurt in the process. There is some good in Benji deep down inside of him somewhere. I know because I saw it. Our first few months together were magical. He just got in with this bad crowd and has been influenced in a negative way. This is not the real Benji. But he's in there somewhere. I just have to dig him out. And I'm determined I won't stop until I do. I just hope it doesn't kill me in the process.

CHAPTER 18

March 5, 2013

The last few months have been going really good. I think Benji's arrest was a real wake-up call. As soon as he was released, he called me crying, begging, apologizing. He swore he would do whatever it took to make things right. He swore to never put his hands on me again. He swore he would get it together. And so far, he has. He has stopped hanging out with the bad group of friends. He's spending more time with me. He actually seems really happy, like all the time, almost a little too happy. Honestly, something still seems a little off, but I'm trying to give him the benefit of the doubt and not make any assumptions or accusations. I just want to put all this behind us and move forward. We have dinner reservations tonight at a really nice restaurant downtown. I'm really excited about it. We haven't been on an actual date night since a couple of months after we got married. I slip on a sleek burgundy dress and black heels and sit on the couch to wait for Benji. He was supposed to be here at four-thirty and it's almost five. I'm starting to get nervous since our reservation is at six, and he's still not here and not answering his phone. I try one more time, still no answer. Finally, at five-thirty, he busts through the door, anger smeared all across his face. "Benji, what's wrong? Where have you been? We're going to miss our reservations."

He walks right past me in one swift motion, acting as if he doesn't hear or see me standing there talking to him.

"Just get in the car." He storms to the bedroom and then returns with a clean shirt. I walk out of the door and head to the car and he follows behind me. He doesn't speak to me the whole way there. I fight back tears, wanting to tell him to just forget it and turn around and go home, but I'm scared to say anything right now. He's driving way too fast, and I close my eyes and hold my breath in fear that we may crash. We pull up at the restaurant at 6:10 p.m. and I'm sure they will turn us away, but surprisingly, they show us to our seats. Benji orders a glass of whiskey and sucks it down within seconds. My eyes widen as I watch him.

"Benji, slow down. We're just having dinner."

He slams the empty glass down on the table and looks around the room like an angry wolf searching for prey. Suddenly, it hits me. He's craving something, something that he's had that suddenly he doesn't. That's why he was late because he was out looking for it. And that's why he's been so happy lately and he's so angry now. That happiness wasn't real. It was a high, and now he's having withdrawals from whatever it was. I clench my fists under the table. Suddenly, his phone starts to chime repeatedly. He picks it up and looks at the screen and his eyes immediately light up. He jumps up from the table and looks frantically around the room.

"I have to go." He pushes his chair back and tosses his credit card across the table at me. "Just order me whatever you're having. I'll be back in thirty minutes." I jump up from the table and grab his arm as he steadily walks away from me.

"Benji? What? Are you freaking kidding me? You're just going to leave me here. Are you crazy?" I continue to pull on his arm, begging him to just sit down.

"Let go, Julia! I'll be right back. Stop being such a baby."

He jerks his arm from me, and I continue to go after him. Suddenly, his hand is going violently against my face and he is pushing harshly into my chest. I fall back into the wall as he exits the restaurant and disappears from my sight. My face starts to sting intensely. My back aches, and once again, the breath is knocked out of me. I don't even cry this time. I just sit there on the floor, emotionless. Several people gather around me. One man pulls me up and asks if I'm okay. The waiter brings me water and helps me back to my seat. I have literally never been so humiliated in my entire life. I don't even have to call the cops this time. The restaurant manager calls and reports the incident.

Just a few hours ago, I was thinking that I would be spending a romantic dinner with my husband. Instead, I'm sitting at the restaurant alone, talking to a cop, giving the physical description of Benji and his vehicle. My stomach turns. How dumb I was to think that things were better. The cop offers to give me a ride home, but I don't go home. I go to Anna's, even though I know the look she will give me, even though I know I will break her heart once again. At least I know I will be safe.

A couple of hours later, I get a call from the police station. They inform me that Benji has been arrested. He was in possession of cocaine and resisted arrest on the scene. This time, I feel like I just might leave him. But I'm still not sure. I still don't know if I'm strong enough to leave. Yet I don't know if I'm strong enough to stay either. Sometimes I wish that I could just forget that Benji ever even existed.

CHAPTER 19

April 17, 2013

I stand frozen in the bathroom, staring at those two lines. They stare boldly back at me with their reddish-pink tint, daring me to question their existence. My hand trembles as it weakly grips the white plastic stick that they call home. A single tear rolls down my cheek and I quickly wipe it away, telling myself that I have to toughen up. It's not just me that I have to look out for now. But honestly, how in the world does a baby fit into this hot mess of a life I have made for myself? Will this cause Benji to truly change? Or will he take me and our child right down the drain with him as he continues to spiral? The thought takes my breath away. I hear the front door shut, so I quickly wrap the test in toilet paper and shove it as far down into the trash can as possible, making sure that it is no longer in sight. *I could just disappear*, I think to myself. I could leave, and he would never have to know anything about this baby. But then I remind myself that this child is not just mine. It's his too. And even if Benji has been a total loser for most of the time we have been married, he has a right to know his kid. And then there's this whole thing where I just can't seem to leave him either. I love him too much. Even if he treats me like the dirt he crushes under his shoes when he walks, I love him. I have to tell him tonight.

I walk into the kitchen and start prepping for dinner. Benji stumbles past me, whiskey hot on his breath. I try to act as if I don't notice.

"Spaghetti okay?" I try to keep my tone as upbeat as possible.

"Um, yeah. You think you could make something that takes a little more effort than dumping something out of a box for a change, Jules?"

He plops down on the couch and starts to flip through channels. Why do I love him? How stupid can one person be? I deserve better. My baby deserves better. But I have to at least give him a chance to get his shit together and be a good father, even if he is a terrible husband. I decide I can't wait until dinner to tell him. He will only be more drunk by then. I need to tell him now. I need to know how he will respond. I toss the package of pasta across the kitchen counter and walk into the living room, stopping directly in front of him and blocking the TV.

"We need to talk." I cross my arms to show him I mean business.

"Ugh, what now, Julia? What? I'm sorry I made the stupid comment about the damn pasta. Now just move and leave me alone." He throws his head back and covers his face as if he can't stand the thought of looking at me or hearing my voice for one more second.

"Benji, I'm pregnant."

The words hit him like bullets. He stares blankly at me as his mouth hangs limply open. Finally, he starts to shake his head and puts his hands up as if he is defending himself against me, against this news, against our unborn child.

"No. Nope. No. You're not. No. Not happening. Nope." He stands up and brushes past me.

"What do you mean not happening? It IS happening, Benji. I AM pregnant. I just took a test."

"No, Jules. Just no. I can't deal with this right now, okay? My parents just cut me off. I don't even know how I'm going to make money now. I can't deal with a kid, not right now. I'm sorry."

He walks to the kitchen, grabs his keys, and heads toward the door.

"Benji, stop! What does that even mean? If you don't want anything to do with us, just tell me and I will pack my stuff and leave and you will never hear from me again. But you can't just not accept that I'm pregnant. I am having a baby, our baby, and you need to tell me now if you're in or out."

"I'm out."

He slams the door in my face, and I open it right back up and run after him. "Benji, where are you going? You can't drive right now. You're completely wasted. Just come back inside. We can talk about this later. Please!"

Dust flies in my face and all around me as he speeds off and leaves me standing there, crying helplessly, foolishly in the driveway of our broken home.

I lay curled up in a ball on the couch, crying uncontrollably for hours, waiting for him to come back. He doesn't. I'm not sure what I expected. I shouldn't be surprised. But it still hurts like hell. I guess I was actually dumb enough to believe that this would soften his heart, that it would motivate him to do right, and that he would want us to be a family. Suddenly, my phone rings angrily into the silence of the night. I glance at the screen and see that it is 2:00 a.m. and I don't recognize the number calling. I start to ignore it but then slide it over to answer at the last second.

"Mrs. Harris."

"Yes."

"This is Officer Daley. Your husband has been arrested for driving under the influence. You can come down to the station in the morning to get details on his bail. Do you have any questions until then?"

I shut my eyes and try to pull myself together long enough to end the conversation.

"No. Thank you, officer."

April 18, 2013

I stare at the clock as I tap my finger on the table and sip my coffee. I don't have money to bail Benji out of jail. He just told me his parents cut him off. Do I call and tell them? Do I just let him sit there? He definitely deserves to sit there. Maybe I will. And if the cops call back, I will tell them to contact his parents. That way, I don't have to. I'm not going up there. In fact, the best thing for me to do is just pack my stuff and not be here whenever he does make it back. Once again, my phone interrupts my thoughts and I see the same number from last night lighting up the screen.

"Hello."

"Julia. It's me. I need your help. I've been thinking a lot. I'm so sorry. I love you. And I will love our baby too. I've just been stressed out. I know I didn't react the way I should have. It just caught me off guard. I promise I want to do better for you and our kid. I want to be a better husband and an even better father. I got this, Jules. I can do better. But first, I just need you to get me out of here. Please. Call my parents. Tell them about the baby. That will soften them up and they will pay my bail. Please. Just tell them I got stressed because of money and finding out you were pregnant. They will help me. I know it."

Why does he always have to reel me back in? While he's out doing actual drugs, he doesn't even realize he's my drug. No matter how hard I try to break away, he sucks me back in and the addiction takes control. I take a deep breath and wipe away a single tear as it rolls quickly down my cheek.

"Okay, Julia? You there?"

"Yeah."

I hang up and call his parents, even though I still feel like he deserves to sit there and rot. They agree to help him. But they warn me that this is the last time, even with the baby coming. They tell me that they are on the verge of ending all contact with Benji for good. They tell me that they hope he will change, but if he doesn't, I should also end things with him. They tell me they are worried about me and now also for my child. They tell me that their son is not good for anyone. Their words cut me like glass.

I can't even think about telling Anna any of this, even though I know she will probably find out. But I do want to tell her that I'm pregnant. I decide to pack a bag, drive up for a visit, and get away from Benji for a couple of days. Maybe if I'm not here when he gets home, he will realize that he really could lose me.

CHAPTER 20

June 10, 2013

For the last couple of months, I have really stood my ground with Benji. I have removed all hard liquor from our home. I have demanded that he get his life in order if he ever wants to see his child and I have banned his loser friends from coming anywhere near us. I want to say things are looking up. I want to say we are making progress and moving forward. But I can't honestly say that. Something is still not right. Something is still off.

He seems so distant in a way I've never seen him before. He's pale and empty, almost like a ghost. His eyes are sunken in and encircled with dark, deathly rings. When I look into them, I see no emotion, no happiness, no anger—just nothing. His pupils are almost nonexistent.

Even though it's the middle of summer, he constantly wears long sleeves. How could he possibly be cold? I just can't make any sense of it. But I'm also afraid to question any of it. At least he's not so angry anymore. At least he's not getting arrested or running around getting into trouble.

He's always here, but at the same time, he never really is. I feel so alone, so trapped, so afraid and confused. I am living with a stranger, with a vapor in the wind that occasionally passes me in the hallway.

I want to leave but continue to stay. I can't seem to force my way through the front door of this sad, pathetic, lonely life I live. What will the future hold for me? And even more importantly, what will the future hold for my child? To be honest, I'm completely terrified of the future. It is dark and angry as it stares me down and dares me to come toward it. I continue to turn and will it away, but I know that I cannot continue to deny the reality that is coming for me.

Eventually, I will have to make a decision for me, for my baby. I will have to either commit to staying or leaving. And no matter what I decide, I lose and so does my baby. It's just not fair, this card of life that we have been dealt. Why me? Why us? Why was I never worthy of true love? My father never loved me and neither will Benji.

I feel so pathetic as I face the truth that I have already failed my child in the few short months he or she has been growing inside of me. I failed from the start simply based on the fact that Benji is the father. I set myself and my child up for destruction, and now it's too late to change it, too late to make it right or take it back. If only I had listened to the one person who ever really did care for me. Anna tried to warn me, but I was just too stubborn, blinded by young, new love. And now this is where it has gotten me. Just pathetic, foolish, stupid. My father was absolutely right about me, and now my child will pay the price for my own ignorance.

CHAPTER 21

June 11, 2013

Anna

My sister has become a zombie. Ever since she showed up on my doorstep two months ago and told me she was pregnant, it has been like she disappeared from the planet. I mean, I know I may have not been the most supportive person ever, but it's only because I fear for her future, for her life. I'm completely terrified for her. Not only is she married to this asshole but now she's having his baby. I just can't process it all. This means that I now have two other lives to look after and protect besides my own and I'm not even a parent.

I tried so hard to steer Julia down the right path and look where it has gotten me. We barely even talk anymore. She has become completely withdrawn and reclusive. She called me this morning to say that Benji was caught with heroin late last night. She doesn't even sound upset. She doesn't sound angry. She doesn't sound anything, just empty. He has completely sucked the life out of her and turned her from happy and cheerful to miserable, empty, and defeated.

I feel like I am going crazy worrying about her. I feel like I have worried myself to the point I can't even function anymore. Maybe I should just give up all together. Maybe I should just go crazy and be the kid I never got the chance to be. Maybe I should just be the irresponsible one for once.

But then that would make others suffer.

And I would be to blame. And that's not me. So I will continue fighting for the ones I love the most, for Julia, and now for her baby too. I will do whatever it takes to protect them. With every ounce of life that is left in me, I will make sure they are safe.

But if I need to make someone else suffer in the process to do so, then I will. And I'm starting to think that I'm inching closer and closer to that point. Benji has caused so much pain for my sister. And now he will cause pain to this baby. He needs to be dealt with. He is toxic energy in this world, a waste of space, an evil force that inflicts pain and suffering to the innocent.

He must be stopped.

CHAPTER 22

June 22, 2013

Julia

I'm tossing and turning, my body at war with my mind. I'm so exhausted, physically and emotionally. This pregnancy has sucked the life out of me and so has my relationship with Benji. All I want to do is keep sleeping, but I'm so restless. I reach across the bed and realize that Benji is no longer lying beside me, which only intensifies my restlessness. I'm not sure how I will be able to handle a baby when I already feel like I am constantly taking care of a child. Where could he be? Why would he be up this early? It's barely daylight outside. There is no reason for him to be up already.

I get up and walk to the bathroom. If I am going to have to go on a search mission, I'm at least going to pee first. I flip on the dimmer light that shines over the shower, careful not to attack my still-tired eyes with too much brightness. But suddenly, something stops me in my tracks, something that makes my heart beat furiously in my chest and causes my blood to suddenly burn inside my veins. I gasp for air and grab the doorframe for support, desperately trying to steady my balance as my body sways back and forth.

"Benji."

His name leaves my lips in a shaky, terrified whisper. I gather myself enough to run to him as the whisper turns to screams. I drop to my knees and frantically start to shake his lifeless body. A shiny, silver needle hangs from his arm. I jerk it out and check his pulse. He's alive.

Suddenly, he wakes up and grabs my arm, staring at me wildly.

"Jules, what happened? Where are we?"

It is in this very moment that I know we cannot continue like this. I am no longer strong enough to try to save Benji on my own. I have tried and I have failed. I have to get him professional help, for him, for myself, for our child.

CHAPTER 23

June 23, 2013

After a night in the hospital and talking to several rehab facilities, I have made arrangements for Benji to start a three-month program. His check-in time is tomorrow morning at 10:00 a.m. The hospital is releasing him so we can go home and pack his things tonight.

Thankfully, he didn't overdose this time. He just passed out. He was pumped full of fluids and has already started the detox process. Needless to say, he is completely miserable. But he did agree to go to rehab. I threatened that this was his last chance. And I meant it. Either he follows through with this and gets clean or he will no longer be a part of mine or my child's life. I pull the car around to the front entrance of the hospital and wait for the nurse to push him out in the wheelchair.

After a silent, tense ride home, I help him out of the car and into the house. I tell him to go lay down and rest while I pack his bags. He barely responds. He looks like an empty shell. He looks like death. Once I'm sure that he's asleep, I get most of his things packed and step out on the back porch to call Anna. I have already told her the plans to admit Benji in the morning. She has convinced me to go stay with her for a while, so I want to let her know around what time I will be arriving at her house. I dial her number and wait for her answer, but just as her voice greets me on the other end, I am startled by the sudden, angry screeching of my Dodge Charger tearing violently down the driveway. I drop my phone and run through the house and to the front door, just in time to see my car disappear from sight with Benji at the wheel. I stand there shocked, waiting for the car to reappear, and when it doesn't, I know I must be a complete idiot to have ever thought it would. I walk slowly back to retrieve my phone and find Anna screaming my name, wanting to know what happened.

"He's gone. Anna, he just left in my car. He's running. He's not going to go. He probably never was."

"Oh, Julia. I am so, so sorry. I really did want this to work. Do you want me to come get you? Please just let me come get you," she pleads.

"No. I have to wait here, just in case he comes to his senses, just in case he comes home."

But he doesn't. The next several hours consist of me waiting by the door, like a puppy waiting for its owner. I sit there, holding my phone, waiting for him to return the endless amount of calls I have attempted, jumping at every little sound, thinking it's him. But it's not. He's not coming back, at least not tonight. Finally, I give up hope and decide to go to bed.

CHAPTER 24

December 17, 2013

All this time, I thought Benji was the love of my life. Benji, who is nowhere to be found right now, was nowhere to be found the last fifteen hours that I have fought, struggled, and pushed to bring our daughter into this world. In fact, Benji has been nowhere to be found for about three days now. But honestly, as I look down at my perfect daughter, I no longer care where he is. I don't care what he's doing. He no longer matters. *She* is what matters. She is the love of my life, not him.

I named her Audrey Elayne Harris. Already, she wears my mother's name proudly, confidently. She's strong. I can already see it. She is strong like her Aunt Anna and not weak like her mother. But I'm going to do better. I'm going to become stronger for her. She is so worth it. And Benji is so not.

"Hey, Mommy. How are you feeling?" Anna peeks slowly around the door, whispering so she doesn't wake Audrey.

"Better than I ever have in my entire life."

I smile and motion her over to come sit on the bed beside me, which is where she stayed the whole entire time I was in labor. She was my rock. And honestly, if Benji would have been here instead of Anna, I don't think I would have survived.

"I brought you some more clothes and the bag you had packed for Audrey," she says, handing me literally everything that I have been needing.

I had not thought to grab much before I left for the hospital. I was home alone when my water broke, and after endless unsuccessful attempts of reaching Benji, I finally gave up and called Anna.

Although I feel stupid now for not just calling her in the first place. By the time she made it there, my contractions were getting really close together and we both panicked and left without thinking to grab much of anything.

Later in the evening, Anna makes a trip down to the cafeteria to get some dinner. The lights are off in my room, and Audrey is sleeping in her bed next to mine. I have felt exhausted all day, so I decide to take advantage of the quiet moment and lay my head back and close my eyes. Just as I feel my body giving in to the sleep that it has been craving all day, my eyes suddenly jolt back open at the commotion going on down the hall. I hear several nurses gradually raising their voices and arguing and a man arguing back.

"Just let me see her!" he yells. I hear his fists slam on the counter. "Where the hell is she? Just tell me! Now!"

I think to myself, *What a jerk. Doesn't he know there are newborn babies and exhausted new mothers trying to sleep?*

But as the voice approaches and gets closer and closer, it becomes more and more familiar. And then I realize it's Benji.

First, I'm filled with humiliation for the way that he is acting and the scene that he is causing right in the middle of the maternity ward of a hospital. But then I look around and suddenly feel helpless and vulnerable and my humiliation turns to fear as I realize that I am alone in the room with Audrey. I'm so sore and weak from giving birth that I can barely stand. And Benji is heading straight for us. I have no idea what state he is in, what drugs are in his system, and what he is capable of. What if he tries to hurt me? What if he tries to take Audrey?

Suddenly, my whole body fills with adrenaline and I look frantically around the room, preparing to defend myself. Just as I'm realizing that there is nothing in my reach that could be used as a weapon, the door busts wide open and Benji freezes in the doorway. I freeze also as I wait for his next move. But he doesn't lunge at me. He doesn't go toward Audrey. In fact, he does the exact opposite of what I expect. He drops his head into his hands and begins to sob. At first, they are small, soft sobs. But they become increasingly louder as he makes his way toward me.

"Julia, I am so sorry."

His words come through his sobs. He goes on to tell me that his phone had died. He just now made it home. He doesn't even explain how he knew where I was, but I'm assuming his parents told him.

He grabs my hand and looks me straight in the eyes. "Can I please meet my daughter?"

At first, I hesitate. I feel a little disgusted with his pathetic display of emotions and his ridiculous excuses for being out of reach for several days and completely missing the birth of our child. But then my hormones start racing and I, too, start to tear up a little. And I am really anxious for him to meet her. Surely, once he lays eyes on her, he will be ready to change. How could he possibly see her and not want to do better?

"Just take a quick look," I say. "She's sleeping right now."

I'm still not comfortable with him holding her until I can confirm that he is sober. He walks slowly over to her and looks down. His hands go back to his face and he starts to sob harder. "She's so beautiful, just like you," he says, wiping tears away.

Now I feel extremely confident that he's high. He's never that nice.

I tell him that we will be dismissed to go home the next day. And the only way we will go home with him is if he agrees to take a drug test and passes. He says he will. About that time, I see Anna slowly approaching the door. She stops dead in her tracks as soon as she sees Benji. She steps to the side, out of my sight for about thirty seconds, before entering the room. I know what she's doing. She's gathering herself, trying to convince herself not to go completely off at Benji because she knows it will only make me angry with her. And she's not wrong. I love my sister and I appreciate everything she does for me. But sometimes I have to fight my own battles and it's taken a lot to make her realize that. I feel my stomach turn as she comes back around the corner and into the room. She stares a hole through Benji and takes a seat on the sofa in the corner of the room. She doesn't say a word. No one does for what seems like forever. Finally, Benji says that he's going home to get a shower and he will be back in the morning. I'm not sure I believe him, but right now, all I want is him out of this room and away from Anna. She is really starting to get a crazy look in her eyes when it comes to Benji, a look I don't recognize, a look that scares me a little. The less those two are around each other, the better for everyone.

CHAPTER 25

December 24, 2013

After almost a whole week of being home with Audrey and having absolutely no help from Benji, I decided to pack us up and stay at Anna's for a few days and spend Audrey's first Christmas here with her. I don't know how Benji managed to pass the drug test at the hospital because his mood has been up and down like a roller coaster all week and I can definitely tell he is on something. My guess is heroin again, but I'm sure he will take anything he can get his hands on. He said he was going to meet us here in the morning to spend Christmas with us, but I'm not going to hold my breath. I want so badly for him to man up and be a father to our daughter. But the first week of her life has shown no change in his behavior and I am really starting to lose hope.

Anna is in the kitchen prepping Christmas Eve dinner. I want so badly to go help her, to laugh and cook together like we always have. But I just don't have the strength. I am physically exhausted from caring for a newborn with no help for the past week and emotionally exhausted from dealing with a piece-of-shit husband for the past year. Audrey squirms and whimpers softly from her bassinet and then thankfully soothes herself back to sleep before I have to get up and tend to her.

I sit back and stare at Anna's perfectly decorated tree as I take in the smells that are making their way into the living room from the kitchen. Scents of Balsam fir, apples, and cinnamon surround me. The fireplace crackles as it sends its warmth to surround me and Audrey. I sigh heavily and take in the feelings, the feeling of being home. Anna has always been home for me. A bittersweet emotion consumes me as I wonder if Benji could ever feel like home for me and Audrey. I'm thankful for Anna, but I want so desperately for Audrey to have her father in her life.

But as soon as I allow my mind to drift to Benji, the room no longer feels cozy and warm. My blood runs cold and I shiver as I think back over all the hell that man has put me through. If I'm being honest, I hope he doesn't show up tomorrow. I hope I don't have to lay another eye on him until Christmas is over. As heartbreaking as it is for me to imagine him missing Audrey's first Christmas, I know that if he is here, he will only ruin it.

CHAPTER 26

June 16, 2014

The last few months have been a bit of a blur. Benji really isn't around much, and I have come to appreciate that more and more since Audrey was born. I used to obsess over where he was all the time. I would worry when he would stay out late at night. I would call his phone repeatedly in desperation for him to come home. But now, things are different. My world revolves around my daughter. I don't really care what Benji does anymore. In fact, I think I have already let go of him emotionally.

Last month, he punched me right in the face and busted my nose while Audrey screamed from her bed just a few feet away. I don't even remember what exactly happened to lead up to it. All I remember is being exhausted from the night before because Audrey had not slept well. We were snappy with each other. And before I knew it, I was on the floor, holding my nose as blood gushed through my fingers and onto my shirt. He disappeared for about a week after that and then returned with flowers. I tossed them in the sink and walked past him as if he wasn't there.

I had not planned to tell Anna, but she dropped by unexpectedly later that day and saw my bruised, swollen face, so I had to fess up. Of course, she begged me to leave him. And of course, I made excuses for him because that's what I do.

I'm pathetic. I'm lost and I am broken. I told her I loved him, but honestly, I don't think I do at this point. I have become completely lifeless. I'm too tired to leave and I'm too tired to stay. I'm just here. I sometimes wonder if Audrey senses my emptiness, if she knows her mother is worthless and incapable of walking away from a man who beats her. I wonder if she will be disgusted with me when she gets older and she knows that I kept her here in an abusive home.

"What if it's the baby next time, Julia?" Anna had said to me that day. Well, I know one thing: If he ever lays a finger on my daughter, I will murder him with my own two hands. But I just haven't worked up the strength to go running to Anna, head held low, standing at her door with everything I own surrounding me, including my daughter, saying, "Okay, Anna. You were right. I shouldn't have married him. I should have gone to college. You were right and I was wrong. I failed. Now since I screwed my own life up, can me and my child come live with you and screw yours up too, just like I always have? After you literally sacrificed your whole childhood, your whole future, your whole life for me, can I come crash on your couch, eat all your food, and continue to take everything you have?"

Yeah, I'm not quite ready to do that, not just yet. I'm really hoping there is another way out of this.

CHAPTER 27

August 8, 2014

Anna

My hand trembles as I hold a small photograph and try to fight back tears. I look into the three smiling faces staring back at me and think back to the day the picture was taken. My beautiful mother has one arm wrapped around each of us. She beams with joy as mine and Julia's heads both tilt toward hers. I remember the day clearly because it was one of the rare days that my stepdad was not so horrible. In fact, he was the one that snapped the photo, saying, "Let me get a shot of my three gorgeous girls."

We had been to the park and then to the local diner for hamburgers and milkshakes. They had even let us stay up late that night to watch a movie. It was one of the few good memories of our childhood. Even though all memories of my mother were good, most of them were tainted by my stepfather's emotional and physical abuse. There just weren't that many good or happy days for any of us. But this particular day was good. And we just so happened to have a picture to prove it.

I run my finger across Julia's tiny smiling face and wonder if I will ever see her smile like that again. I don't even recognize her anymore. She has become vacant. Benji has stolen her joy and I'm not sure she will ever get it back. For that to ever even be possible, she would have to at least leave him. But it doesn't look like that is going to happen.

I'm starting to grow extremely impatient. I have watched Benji destroy my sister for far too long. I tried to respect her wishes. I tried to back off and let her handle things. But she is not handling things, not even a little bit. And now she has a baby. I can't just sit back and watch him tear them both down. I did what I had to do to get her away from her father, and now I will do what I have to do to get them both away from Benji.

I'm done playing nice. I gave her a chance to leave, countless chances. I gave him countless chances to change. I have had enough. It's time for angry Anna to come out and set things straight. She has been locked away long enough. I can't contain her anymore. She must be set free to settle the score. Benji has to go. And he has to go soon, very soon. My sister's life is dangling by the seconds. I just know that if I don't end him, he will end her. He will literally kill her if I don't do something to get rid of him. So really, it is defense. I mean, who wouldn't kill to protect their own family? Anyone would go to extreme measures to protect those that they love.

Benji doesn't deserve to live. He deserves to suffer. He deserves to feel the pain that he has caused others. And he will much sooner than later.

CHAPTER 28

September 23, 2014

Here it is, all laid out in front of me: my plan to kill Benji. It's the perfect plan, really. No one will ever suspect foul play. No one will question why he wrecked his car because everyone knows that he stays high out of his mind all the time. And the best part is I don't actually have to do any dirty work. I think if it came down to actually, physically taking someone's life with my own hands, I would freak and back out. But this way, I just kind of have to pave the road that leads him to dying.

Once I have done my part, it is no longer in my hands. I feel like I have thought of everything to cover myself. I'm even going to offer to keep Audrey that night so that Julia won't have to worry about taking care of her when she first hears the bad news. I'm going to have Gracie come over and watch her while I run my errand.

Everything is all set up. I have spent the last month sneaking around, learning what times Benji comes and goes the most. I have followed him to see where he goes at what times. I pretty much know his whole routine at this point. But soon, his routine will be disrupted. His life will be disrupted, just like he disrupted ours. I tried to warn him to stay away from my sister from the start. If he would have just listened, it would have never come to this. But now I have no choice. He has to go.

CHAPTER 29

September 27, 2014

Once I have Audrey all settled in at my house with Gracie, I quietly slip out of the front door. Gracie doesn't know where I'm going or what I'm about to do, but I could see the suspicion in her eyes. She knows me too well to not know that I'm up to something. She didn't ask questions. She just hugged me tightly before I walked out and told me to be safe. I know that once she hears about Benji, she will know I had something to do with it. But Gracie is that friend that I can trust without a single doubt. She won't ask questions just so she doesn't have to lie for me if it comes down to it. She can truly say she doesn't know anything.

My whole body is shaking as I race toward Benji and Julia's house. I play the last couple of years over and over in my head, reminding myself that I'm doing the right thing. "Even his own parents don't want anything to do with him," I tell myself. All he does is cause pain for others. He has had it coming for a long time.

Finally, I arrive to their home, but I don't pull into the driveway. I pull to the side of the road, hiding my car as much as possible. Fully dressed in black so I'm sure not to be seen, I sprint across the yard carrying a can of gasoline, a pair of wire cutters, and a small flashlight. It just so happens that I know the locks on Benji's truck don't work, so that won't be an issue. I quietly open the driver's side door, bend down to the floor, and shine the light toward the brake pedal. I grab the wire cutters and reach behind the pedal, cutting the bright-red wire with one solid snip. I then sprinkle some of the gasoline directly onto the seat where Benji will be sitting in just a few minutes. I take a long, deep breath, quietly shut the door, and make my way back to my car. Now all I can do is wait. I won't wait for the whole thing, but I just want to see for sure that he does leave when I expect him to, which is in about thirty minutes.

95

CHAPTER 30

September 27, 2014

Julia

I was so thankful when Anna offered to watch Audrey for me for the night. I have been desperate for a break lately. But now that she's gone, I realize how little of a life I have without her. I need the break, but I need to be with her more. I just miss her so much already, but I'm also missing Anna, so I decide to crash their sleepover and stay the night too. Benji will be leaving soon anyway to go wherever the hell it is that he goes every night around this time. I pack a small bag and head for the front door. He is already stirring in the kitchen, obviously getting ready to head out too.

"Going to Anna's," I say as I'm walking out of the door, shutting it behind me before he has a chance to respond. I pull my jacket tightly around me as a cool September breeze blows over me, and suddenly, chills run down my spine as I try to shake the uneasy feeling that someone is watching me. I shrug off the thought, telling myself that I'm being ridiculous, and hop into my car, shutting the door as quickly as possible. I'm sure I will feel better once I'm on the road with the radio blaring, except that doesn't happen because my car doesn't start. I turn the key repeatedly, pleading with it to just work. "Damn it!" I hit the steering wheel and drop my head into my hands.

About that time, Benji comes out of the front door and heads to his truck. I jump out of my car and do the last thing I want to have to do right now.

"Hey, can you give me a ride to Anna's? My car won't start."

He shakes his head slightly, being sure to let me know how much of an inconvenience I am. "Get in," he says sharply without ever looking my way. I roll my eyes, grab my bag from my car, and head to his truck.

"Benji, do you smell gas?"

"I don't know, Julia. Just get in. I don't have time for this shit."

Seriously, why does he have to be such a jerk *all the time?*

About that time, a car horn starts blaring in the distance. I'm pretty sure I can see headlights flashing in the same direction. And they also seem to be approaching us. I start to feel uneasy, but Benji acts as if he doesn't even notice. The car comes at us quicker and quicker as Benji whips the truck out of the driveway and pushes his foot on the pedal, eventually speeding right past the car. I try to distract myself and just think about getting back to Audrey. Soon, she will be in my arms again.

Benji continues to go faster and faster, and suddenly, I realize that the car has turned around and is now behind us, still blaring the horn uncontrollably. I turn around and try to see the vehicle and driver, but their headlights are blinding. Benji seems to grow more and more agitated, and I'm starting to wonder if this is someone he knows, if maybe he is in some kind of trouble.

I turn back around just in time to see a stop sign coming at us much faster than it should be. I then notice Benji beating his foot violently against the brakes. The truck doesn't slow down. It seems to mock him as he continues to battle the brake pedal.

"It won't stop," he yells. "Julia, it won't stop! We're gonna crash!"

I take one last look ahead of us just in time to see a tree heading directly for us. I close my eyes and picture my daughter's face.

CHAPTER 31

Anna

If I didn't know any better, I would swear Julia was climbing into the truck with Benji. *What the hell?* I didn't plan for this. I didn't even slightly consider this as a possibility. She literally never goes anywhere with him anymore. From my understanding, they barely even speak to each other. Why is she climbing into the truck with him? How can this be happening? I have to stop her. I cannot be responsible for killing my own sister!

I do the only thing I know to do and start blowing the horn as hard as I can. I'm racing toward them as fast as I can. I have no idea what I will say if I stop them, but I don't care. I will think of something. I just have to get my sister out of that truck. They pull out of the driveway and race past me like I'm not even here. I immediately pull into their driveway and turn around to catch up with them. I don't let up on the horn as I race down the curvy road until I am on their tail. I'm begging, pleading. Please stop the truck! But then I remind myself that they can't stop the truck. They can't stop because I cut the fucking brakes! Then I see it: the stop sign coming up just ahead of them. They haven't slowed down one bit and they aren't going to because they can't.

I'm screaming now, gripping the steering wheel like it's my lifeline. How could I have done this? How could this have happened? I stay close behind them until there is nowhere left for them to go. I slam on brakes and my heart stops as I watch the truck plummet through the air, crashing directly into a tree and immediately bursting into flames.

My feet are beating against the pavement before I even realize I am out of the car. I'm gasping for air, heart beating in my head. Everything is silent other than the constant pounding in my ears. I fight back the vomit that slowly creeps up my throat. The smell of burning flesh and rubber fills the air as I drag my lifeless sister out of the truck and onto the ground. I'm screaming, crying, making sounds that aren't even human as I frantically check her for a pulse. I sob uncontrollably when I find one. I look over her entire body and see that she doesn't seem to be burned. I got to her before the fire did. But the cut on her head makes me queasy, and I still question if she will be okay as I see the blood start to gush uncontrollably from her forehead.

All this time, I have been trying to save her from Benji, but now I have hurt her far worse than he ever did. And then I remember Benji.

I glance up at the truck and it doesn't take but a split second to know that he is gone. And suddenly, I feel like the most disgusting and horrific person to ever walk the face of the earth.

CHAPTER 32

September 28, 2014

I sit frozen in the waiting room of the emergency room, with Julia's dried blood covering my body. This is where I have sat for the past twelve hours, waiting, crying, wondering what the hell to do. I have heard the words coma, possible memory loss, bleeding on the brain. They all run together, just like the seconds, minutes, and hours have. I don't know where to go from here. I don't know how to move. I don't know how to breathe. I don't know how to live in a world without Julia in it, especially if I am the one that took her out of it. I had panicked and told the doctors that I was on my way to visit her when I happened to see her wandering down the street with a bloody head. I told them that she had lost consciousness on the way to the hospital. I hoped my lie would not prevent them from treating her condition properly, but I could not risk them questioning how I just so happened to be present at the time of the wreck.

Eventually, a nurse walks me to a room to speak with the doctor again. She brings me a fresh cup of coffee, and I am determined that I am going to fully process everything he tells me this time. After hours of nodding and acting as if I am comprehending the details they are giving me, this time, I have to pull myself together and truly make myself understand what is going on with Julia.

The doctor shakes my hand and smiles kindly. He tells me that Julia is being kept in a medically induced coma to allow time for the fluid on her brain to lessen and the swelling to go down. He says that hopefully, she will be able to wake up in a couple of days, but even if she does, there is a very good chance she could have lost all memory. I gasp for air as I feel the panic taking over my body. The doctor tells me that Julia will need me to be stable—that she will need me to handle whatever state of mind she wakes up in without being hysterical. He tells me that she doesn't need any extra stress, that she doesn't need to be told right away that her husband was killed, and that she doesn't need any upsetting news until she is strong enough to handle it. He says to just give her time and find out where she is at mentally before giving her any kind of information. I sit silently long after he is gone and let the words that he spoke bounce around in my mind as I try to grasp them individually. It is then that I realize that I have to make a decision. I have to make a plan. I have to be prepared for either outcome. I have to be prepared for if she remembers and also if she doesn't. One thing that I do know is that if she doesn't remember anything, she can't even know that Benji existed. I can't risk her knowing what I did. But if she doesn't know that Benji existed, that means she also can't know that Audrey is hers. In fact, if she doesn't remember anything or anybody, then maybe it's best she doesn't even know who I am. Maybe I should just start fresh with her, somehow become her friend. I don't want to lie to her but I have to cover up what I did, at least for now until we see if her memory is going to come back. After all that has happened, it is important that I protect her now more than ever.

CHAPTER 33

September 30, 2014

My stomach turns as I stuff my sister's whole entire life into a small metal box.

I pack away her wedding picture with Benji, photos of her and Audrey, and her wedding rings that they had slipped off her finger at the hospital and put into a plastic bag labeled, "Patient's belongings." Lastly, I pick up the photo of me, Julia, and our mother. I hold it tightly to my chest as I struggle to fight back tears.

"Goodbye, Julia."

I shove the picture into the box and shut it.

I head back to the hospital and prepare for the worst.

Gracie has agreed to stay with Audrey as much as possible, and when she isn't able to, the sweet lady a few houses down will watch her until I can find a way to bring Julia home and care for both of them here. For now, I will be spending most of my time at the hospital.

October 10, 2014

Julia woke up a little over a week ago. The doctors were right. She doesn't remember anything, not me, not Audrey, not Benji, not even herself. I managed to convince her that I am a nurse and have been assigned to sit with her daily. She's confused and completely clueless about everything right now, so she didn't question it at all. I have also convinced her to come home with me. She was completely terrified when she found out she was being released from the hospital, which was the perfect opportunity for me to swoop in and save the day and get her right where I need her—in my home under my constant care.

The nurses hugged me as we were leaving, telling me goodbye. As long as we have been here, I have gotten somewhat close to most of them. I used this as an opportunity to make it look like they were telling me goodbye because I was taking off work for a while.

As I push Julia down the hallway in a wheelchair, I wonder what her future holds. I wonder if she will ever get her memory back. I wonder if she will ever learn the truth about all the things I have done, all the things I'm doing now. I wonder if she would ever forgive me if she did. I wouldn't blame her if she didn't. After a lifetime of trying desperately to protect her, I think it is safe to say that I failed her in every way possible. And now I have failed her daughter too. Now not only do I have to lie to Julia, but I also have to lie to Audrey when she's older. And I honestly hope the guilt will fade over time because right now, it is literally eating its way through the entirety of my whole heart and soul. I just wish I could undo it all. I wish I could take it all back. But it's too late. The only thing I can do now is move forward.

CHAPTER 34

April 16, 2018

I can't do it anymore. I feel like every ounce of life has been sucked out of me. Things had been going so good but then Julia started digging deeper and deeper and eventually found Benji on the Internet—their wedding announcement, his arrests, all of it. I know this because I have her laptop linked to mine. I gave it to her as a birthday gift a couple of years ago. Something deep inside me just knew that eventually, she would get curious and start digging. And I wanted to be aware of it when she did, so I got it for her and linked it to mine. So if she decided to dig, I could watch and see what she found. And what she has found is not good. She hasn't mentioned any of it to me yet. But she has been acting completely different.

She stays locked in her apartment all the time. She doesn't interact with me and Audrey anymore, and I can't help but wonder if what she found on the Internet triggered some of her memories to come back. I wonder if she knows what I did. I wonder all the time. What does Julia know? That is all I think about ever.

She is on to me. I just know it. And I just can't do it anymore. It is eating me alive. I have to come clean with her. She finally came down for dinner last night after I sent Audrey up with cookies as a desperate attempt to find out what state of mind she's in. The whole night was tense. I felt like she could see right through me. I felt like my skin was burning and she could see the flames. If there is still a chance that she doesn't already know now, I'm to the point I know it's only a matter of time before she finds out. And if she is going to find out, I would rather she hear it from me straight up from the start.

So late last night after she left, I opened the safe in my closet and dug out that metal box that holds all my deep, dark secrets—the box that holds my sister's life. I sat it on the counter and texted Gracie to see if I could bring Audrey to her first thing in the morning. I want to be ready and waiting when Julia wakes up. I am going to tell her everything. If she hates me and never wants to speak to me, that is something I will have to deal with. I have tried to make her decisions for her all her life and look where it got me. Now it is time to lay the truth out in front of her and for once, let her decide what to do with it. I am completely terrified. But I cannot go on like this anymore. She has to hear the truth. And she has to hear it now, all of it.

CHAPTER 35

April 16, 2018

Julia

My whole body is shaking. The amount of traumatic information that my brain has processed in the past hour is more than most people endure in a lifetime. I feel as if I may just float right out of my body. My heart beats wildly in my chest. My mouth turns to cotton, and my throat closes up as I try desperately to swallow. Sweat starts to cover my body, and suddenly, I feel as if I have walked straight into a furnace. My breathing grows more and more unsteady as I try to gather myself enough to figure out how to even begin reacting to Anna.

I'm pacing furiously back and forth, grabbing at my hair, stopping for seconds to look at her, and then continuing to pace again, even faster than before. I try so hard to hold it all in, to handle it like a big girl, and to show Anna that I'm tough, show her that I'm angry, and show her that I won't stand for any of this.

But the scared little girl in me is fighting viciously to reach the surface and I can't contain her anymore. Finally, I give in and back up against the wall, sliding all the way down to the floor. I cry the most pathetic, childish cry imaginable. It grows stronger and stronger as all the feelings connect and intertwine. I feel it all, everything, all at once—years of not knowing who I am or where I came from, years of thinking I had no family, and years of thinking I would never get answers.

And then the pain I felt when I thought I had lost my child is now mixed with the relief of knowing that Audrey is my daughter. A little girl I have loved as my own for the past four years actually is my own. I sob harder as I think of all the time we have missed as mother and daughter but then sob even harder at the thought that she has been there with me all along.

And then Anna's betrayal hits me right in the gut and that's when I fall even further to the floor and cover my head, continuing to cry uncontrollably. It's then that Anna runs over and drops to the floor beside me. She reaches her hand out to me and then draws it back quickly, nervously, not knowing how I will react to her being this close to me. She covers her mouth and starts to cry right along with me. Finally, she just comes right at me and covers me with her whole body, squeezing me tightly.

We stay this way for what seems like forever. I cry until my body simply won't allow anymore. Physically, mentally, emotionally exhausted, I finally pick myself up off the floor, push Anna slightly back, and look her straight in her eyes.

"Anna, take me to my daughter RIGHT NOW."

CHAPTER 36

Julia

We are slowly adjusting to a new normal. There is a big part of me that is still angry with Anna, but I also understand why she did a lot of the things she did. I know that eventually, I will be able to forgive her. I just need time.

Soon, we will have to have a talk with Audrey, explaining that I am really her mother, but for now, we are taking things slowly. We are trying to gradually phase me into being her main caregiver. Anna has backed off and given us more time alone. Eventually, me and Audrey will move out and get a house together. I just don't want to make any movements too soon. I want her to have time to process all this. But honestly, the changes so far haven't even fazed her. I don't even think she has noticed that Anna is no longer the main person taking care of her. I think me and Audrey always still had that bond, a bond that her and Anna never had. They loved each other. And Anna has taken great care of her. But I think even though me and Audrey didn't know our correct titles and relations, our hearts did. Our hearts knew that we were mother and daughter. And that is a bond that can never be broken.

ABOUT THE AUTHOR

Trisha is a first-time author but has always been a writer at heart. She also draws and loves anything art related. Growing up an only child in a small town, she often turned to drawing and writing in her spare time and wrote several short stories throughout her childhood and teenage years. It has always been her dream to pursue a career in art, and as an adult, she finally chose writing to take that path.